Perspectives on Investment Management of Public Pension Funds

Edited by

Frank J. Fabozzi, CFA
Adjunct Professor of Finance
School of Management
Yale University
and
Editor
Journal of Portfolio Management

Robert Paul Molay
Senior Vice President
IMN/Information Management Network

Published by Frank J. Fabozzi Associates

© 1999 By Frank J. Fabozzi Associates
New Hope, Pennsylvania

Cover design and photo by Robert Paul Molay

ISBN: 1-883249-56-2

Printed in the United States of America

Table of Contents

Contributing Authors

Garry M. Allen — Two Rivers Capital Management at Kingsmill, Inc.

Joseph A. Braccia — Miller, Anderson & Sherrerd, LLP/ Morgan Stanley Asset Management

John R. Caswell — Galliard Capital Management

T. Daniel Coggin — TeamVest, LLC

Christopher E. D'Amore — State Street Global Advisors

John A. de Luna — State Street Global Advisors

Frank J. Fabozzi — Yale University

Joshua G. Feuerman — State Street Global Advisors

Bruce I. Jacobs — Jacobs Levy Equity Management, Inc.

Kenneth N. Levy — Jacobs Levy Equity Management, Inc.

Nancy C. Nakovick — Bear Stearns & Co.

Thomas K. Philips — Paradigm Asset Management

Karl P. Tourville — Galliard Capital Management

James F. Ward — Plan sponsor adviser

Preface

The trustee of a public pension fund is responsible for making key decisions that will impact the performance of the fund. Because of the increasingly complex nature of the products traded in today's capital market and the risks associated with the various strategies that are being used by investment managers, typically a trustee will rely on the services of a consultant. Yet, a trustee cannot turn over his or her responsibilities to a consultant because of the complexities associated with managing funds.

The purpose of this book is to provide the perspectives of experts on key topics associated with the investment management of public pension funds. This will help a trustee understand and respond to the issues as they are presented by consultants that are retained by the fund, existing money managers employed by the fund, and potential managers who are being interviewed for engagement.

A major question for public pension funds is whether to manage funds internally or retain the services of an external money manager. In Chapter 1, James Ward discusses the issues associated with internal versus external management. In Chapter 2, Garry Allen and Daniel Coggin explain the challenges of internal management of pension assets. They also provide an organizational structure to meet these challenges.

In Chapter 3, two well-known money managers who have been major contributors to the investment management literature, Bruce Jacobs and Kenneth Levy, explain the key elements of active equity portfolio management and the complexity of the equity market. They then explain a model for selecting stocks.

A public pension fund sponsor must decide whether to pursue an active or passive investment strategy. The chapter by Jacobs and Levy sets forth what a public pension plan sponsor should expect from an active equity manager. If the decision is to allocate funds to the equity market but not follow pursue an active equity strategy, then there are two types of passive strategies. One is a simple buy-and-hold strategy. The other is an indexing strategy and it is this strategy that is the most common form of passive strategy followed by funds. The notion of indexing is that in an efficient market, an investor can capture the efficiency of the market by creating a portfolio that mimics the market. In Chapter 4, Thomas Philips explains the advantages and disadvantages of indexing and the interplay between active management and indexing.

There is a wide range of strategies that can be employed by public pension plans. These strategies are reviewed in Chapter 5 by Nancy

Nakovick. The strategies she discusses not only address how to reduce the problem of underfunding, but they allow a sponsor to maintain above-average market returns during periods of above-average market volatility. Also of concern to the plan sponsor is the use of derivatives beyond that of risk-control strategies. She explains how these instruments can be used effectively by plan sponsors.

One of the asset classes from which a public pension fund sponsor can allocate funds to is international equities. In Chapter 6, Christopher D'Amore and Joshua Feuerman present the case for international investing. They look at whether international diversification can be obtained by simply holding U.S. companies that do business overseas. If a public pension fund sponsor elects to invest in international equities, the next question is whether or not to hedge currency risk. In Chapter 7, Joseph Braccia reviews the issues associated with hedging currency risk and the empirical evidence addressing this question.

In Chapter 8, John de Luna looks at traditional approaches to cash management and dispels some of the myths about cash management. Specifically, he challenges the popular notion that short-term investment funds are the best and least expensive repository for cash. He proposes separate account management as a more prudent and lower-cost alternative.

When a public pension fund sponsor offers a defined contribution plan, it must provide various investment options. One popular investment options is a stable value investment. In Chapter 9, John Caswell and Karl Tourville review the various stable value instruments — traditional guaranteed investment contracts (GICs) and GIC alternatives — and contract terms.

— Frank J. Fabozzi

James F. Ward, CFA, is a plan sponsor adviser and financial consultant with a depth of experience in public funds management.

From 1977 through 1997, Ward was executive director of the Public School Teachers Pension and Retirement Fund of Chicago. In October 1997 he was elected trustee on the government board. He joined the fund as assistant executive director in 1967, at which time it held $200 million in assets.

During Ward's 30-year tenure these assets grew to $8.3 billion and the fund hired 50 money managers and the attorney, actuary, investment consultant, and bank custodian.

His professional experience includes internal and external money management, securities trading, investment policy, evaluation, asset allocation, minority/women representation, directed brokerage, manager search, consultant liaison, and custodian relations.

From 1963 through 1966, Ward taught accounting in Chicago's Kelvyn Park High School and evening classes in small-business management.

Ward is a regular speaker before faculty and retired groups. He is a member of the National Council on Teachers Retirement, the National Conference on Public Employee Retirement Systems, the Government Finance Officers Association, the Security Traders Association of Chicago, the Association of Investment Management, and Research, and the Investment Analysts Society of Chicago. He is a life-long member of the AFL-CIO.

Ward holds a bachelor of education degree in accounting from Chicago Teachers College and a master's degree in business administration, in accountancy, from DePaul University, followed by postgraduate computer studies at Northeastern University (Illinois). He earned his CFA designation at the Institute of Chartered Financial Analysts, University of Virginia.

Chapter 1

Internal Versus External Management

James F. Ward, CFA
Plan Sponsor Adviser
Financial Consultant

You have taken on the thankless task of being a trustee for your public pension fund. Whether you are in the board room or at your mailbox, you ruffle reams of computer printout, multiple asset manager reports, some monthly, some quarterly (which is which?), performance results for 40 managers, each with 40 pages of multiple return tabulations (monthly, quarterly, yearly, and longer). Some are in living color, some not. Some are photocopied into shades of gray.

How many times has a public pension board trustee wondered, "Is there any other way to do this?" This question occurs to trustees with excellent in-house investment staff and to trustees with excellent external managers. When this question is posed it can cause considerable concern to the people on the excellent investment staff or to all the excellent outside managers. This is not to mention the support and resource individuals and firms being utilized in either venue. Whether you have in-house or external management, you also have a retinue of consultants, analysts, account executives, investment bankers, money managers, real estate developers, brokers, accountants, data processors, and others supporting the investment decision makers.

How can the new — or seasoned — trustee ascertain the wisdom of advice received in this context? Will there be a polarity and consequent momentum for whichever type of management is currently in use? Put another way, is it a watershed decision to switch from one type to the other? Whether you have an in-house system or external manager(s), the advice you receive from them will most likely revolve around how wonderful the current system is and how awful the circumstances would be if you were to change to the other system.

To a public pension fund trustee accustomed to one management mode, it may only be a negligible reminder that the other type even exists. But both do, and in considerable size. Nelson's Directory reports that as of 1995 there were over 1,800 internally managed asset pools in the United States with over $1 trillion under their control. This represented about a third of all managed assets in the country. In a study by Vestek Systems Inc. in 1996, it was disclosed that large plans with more than $500 million in assets are most often the primary internal managers, with the public pension systems managing the largest number of dollars internally.[1] Of 171 public plans counted by Nelson's Directory in the 1995 edition, 51 managed money internally with the assets therein representing 50% of all public assets under management. Nelson's goes on to report that, of $921 billion in defined benefit public plans, $624 billion or 68% was internally managed. As might be expected, various corporate, public, foundation, and endowment plans have both internal and external management functions. For the majority of plan participants in the United States that have one plan or the other, this might seem to be an ungainly hybrid. What are the reasons why a plan would take the trouble to do both? Further, is there any evidence that either form is preferable and, if so, under what circumstances?

DETERMINING FACTORS

It is the experience of this writer to have participated as a plan sponsor in both internal and external institutional asset management over three decades. The first type utilized a single balanced manager with a considerable internal operation to implement the investment programs as recommended by the single manager — screened, ratified, and executed by internal procedures. The second type of asset management over the last decade is described as multiple external manager array, selected to implement the sponsor-selected asset-class mix. This second method of operation is widely used by public pension plans in the United States. (See the compilation of the National Council on Teacher Retirement roster of small and large teacher funds,[2] which shows internal and external assets managed by over 30 plans. Also, a cursory perusal of *Money Market Directory*[3] shows the extent to which various public and corporate sponsors used internal and external managers.)

Pertinence in Large Asset Pools

Usually, the internal-versus-external issue is deemed most pertinent in the management of large asset pools, particularly public plans. It is offered here that this may not be the case. The basic operational and economic considerations that come into play may have corresponding rele-

---

[1]"Managing Money In-House," Vestek Systems Inc. (San Francisco: 1996).
[2]Austin, Texas, 1997.
[3]Division of Standard & Poor's, McGraw-Hill, 1997.

vance to the largest and smallest investors. It will be up to each owner or fiduciary to determine whether and where such a position is suitable for practical application. There are ample compilations of the large asset pools that use internal and external mangers as well as the billions of dollars they manage internally and externally (See directories cited earlier in this chapter). What are not so readily available are numbers on the billions that are handled "internally" by the owners. A question raised here is whether the basic separation of ownership from management is the defining criterion for the label "external?"

Traditional Versus Economic Concepts

Anyone near a mutual fund, a public pension plan, an investment consultant, or investment banker will know of the existence of asset managers. Today, asset managers advertise on prime-time television. It has been said that there are more mutual funds than stocks on the New York Stock Exchange and the only Americans who do not own mutual fund shares are a declining percentage of the homeless. In such terms, all of these managers are "external"from the perspective of owners of the assets, individual mutual fund shareholders, or the institutions that may also be shareholders.

Prudence In a more general sense, the terms "in-house" and "outside" are usually used in the description of how large public asset pools are run. In-house management is just about self-defining. For purposes here, "internal" is simply the owners or owner fiduciaries making investment decisions with or without the help of hired analysts, traders, accountants, or other professionals. Usually, especially with large asset pools, sponsors install a staff and place in them the responsibility for day-to-day implementation of the investment program. Here the definition of "prudent" runs into the circular definition of "prudence" usually applied under statutory and common law: A fiduciary must act for the sole benefit of the beneficiaries of the trust and do so in the same manner as like fiduciaries would act in like circumstances with like assets and liability structures. Of course, such criteria may make for herd manifestations as "like" managers simply do what everyone else is doing.

Know Thyself Such timidity can work to distract the fiduciary from the primary task of designing the investment program to the long-term needs of the specific beneficiary group. The public pension plan sponsor must know itself. The range of assets in the thousands of asset pools existing in the world can only be finally determined by the needs, attitudes, tastes, mores, laws, and politics of the owners. The internal and external manager must begin by asking such questions as: How much do you have? What revenue will you collect? When must you spend it? How? Understanding of the capital markets and asset class options open to the plan will dictate the ultimate success of the investment methodology, its articulation, and its execution. Actuarial requirements, liability calculations, liquidity schedules, duration analyses, demographic influences, diversification advantages, multiple return projections, and political realities will provide the input for the final investment program. Pension plan portfolios are all different, yet they often move together, doing the same things at the same times. This should not be so. The investment program should not retreat from the advantage of custom-tailoring to the safety of average performances.

External Perspective Similar considerations emerge with the various types of external management. Objectives and guidelines are established for each external manager that take into account the primary market within which the manager is charged to invest and, in some cases, a secondary market or style index is used to evaluate the particular market factors which influence investment return. Investment results are compared with like groups of investment managers to provide competitive analysis. Varying time periods are used to judge the success of investment managers during different market conditions, and to evaluate any emerging trends in investment results. Returns should be computed and evaluated both before and after the effect of manager fees.

The 'Horse Race' or Equal Balanced Managers System

Another form of external manager operation differs in an important fashion from the operation described earlier in this chapter. Instead of designing and updating a predetermined asset class mix of something like 45% domestic and global bonds, 45% domestic and global stocks, 10% real estate, or the like — the governing board simply decides on an asset class mix benchmark. Typical choices might be 45% S&P 500 index, 45% Lehman Corporate Government Aggregate Index, and 10% Neicreff or Nareit Real Estate index.

The board selects as many outside managers as it sees fit and compares their investment performances with the benchmark and with each other. Each manager has the freedom to underweight or overweight his asset class mix depending on his own analysis and judgment. Rebalancing or the allocation of new revenues can be made on the basis of relative performance of the external managers. It likely has already occurred to the reader that this system can also be used with an array of external managers and internal managers — with the internal managers providing additional entries in the "horse race."

PERFORMANCE

There have been numerous recent reports indicating that internal performance has been outdoing external performance. *Institutional Investor* regularly polls 250 public pension funds and 800 corporate funds through this publication's "Pensionforum." In its February 1989 survey, *II* found that "36% of respondents use internal operations to manage investments, and nearly 25% say they run more money internally than they did in 1984."[4]

These respondents said internal management is attractive because of more control over performance and lower costs. In a subsequent survey in April 1996, the same publication reported that "by almost all measures, internally managed pension assets outperform those run by outside managers." This survey showed 56% of respondents said their internal portfolios surpassed the S&P 500 or other index. By more than 2-to-1, such portfolios also outperformed the median return for their funds' external equity managers. A whopping 80% reported their in-house equity portfolios outperformed the median return for comparable outside equity managers. Five-year results were similar or better.

With fixed income, the internal portfolios tended to outpace indices while keeping pace with their actual outside fixed advisers. Despite the sterling returns, fewer than one-fourth of the funds do defined-benefits asset management in-house because of the ease of switching managers and the salaries commanded by high-caliber managers. Those that do practice in-house management appear to be loyal believers. A huge majority (almost 73%) say that the amount they manage internally has not changed over the past five years.[5]

The Same or Better?

There do not seem to be any reports in recent years that external managers do better. In 1996, Vestek[6] cited a Cost Effectiveness Measurement Inc. study spanning five years of performance of more than 200 sponsors with assets of $900 billion. The study concluded that the mix of internal and external management did not have a statistically significant effect on

---

[4]"Internal Management Gains Ground," *Institutional Investor* (February 1989): 115.

[5]"In-House Afire," *Institutional Investor* (April 1996): 135.

[6]Vestek Systems Inc., op. cit.

performance before fees. In July 1997 the Cost Effectiveness Measurement study was updated to include 255 funds, of which 155 were American and 95 Canadian, covering $1.3 trillion. This study's findings were summarized as follows:[7]

- Bigger is Better. Larger funds outperformed smaller funds.
- Passive is better. Funds with a higher proportion of passive assets did better.
- Lower cost is better. Funds paying more management fees underperformed.
- Public and corporate performed the same, contrary to popular belief.
- Funds with a higher proportion of internal management have done better than funds with more external management.

This study goes on to suggest the reasons for these findings. It is easier for larger funds to attract and retain the best money managers, both internal and external. In an era of downsizing and outsourcing, one reason used to justify slashing internal operations and using higher-cost external management is to improve performance. "So far, there is no support for this justification. In fact, funds with high proportions of internal management appear to have done better than funds with high proportions of external management."[8]

The Indexing Factor The usual statistical caveat is included here, that recent comparisons favoring in-house over external returns may be due to the fact that much of the internally managed assets are simply indexed. Very few managers have beaten the indices over the last few years during the amazing bull market of the 1990s. Still, pension plans like the giant California Public Employees Retirement System (Calpers) continue to manage a majority of their assets internally and are looking at ways to increase internal aspects of their investment programs.[9]

Dwindling Numbers In a report from the United Kingdom we find another interesting difference. According to the WM Company, British internal pension fund managers substantially outperform external money

---

[7]Tom Scheibelhut, "Characteristics of Top Performing Pension Funds," (July 1997): 2, 5.

[8]Tom Scheibelhut, "Characteristics."

[9]"External vs. Internal," *Pensions & Investments* (March 17, 1997): 10.

mangers but, surprisingly, their numbers are dwindling.[10] These findings, while applying only to the United Kingdom, raise questions for the U.S. industry, which has been sold on the advantages of professional outside managers. European companies are starting to follow the U.S. example and go outside. One key to the better performance of in-house funds is lower portfolio turnover. External teams turn over the whole portfolio once a year; internal managers are half as active.

The British trend seems to be corroborated in the United States, according to Greenwich Associates' survey of 1,600 corporate and public pension and endowment funds. Internal money management shrank sharply between 1994 and 1996 with only 13% of corporate funds and 21% of public funds using internal management.[11]

MANAGEMENT FEES

Depending on the size of reported asset pools counted by Cost Effectiveness Measurement Inc. in the 1995 study, there are considerable savings in management fees. The reduction in costs for active equity management is reported at 25 basis points for portfolios over $5 billion to as much as 38 basis points for portfolios under $1 billion. Fixed-income differentials do not show such magnitude, with a reported 17 to 19 basis points less reported for running bonds internally over externally.

It should be stated that such reported savings must necessarily be based on observations of discrete time periods with individual portfolios reporting. However limited the empirical worth of reported studies, there still remains the reasonableness of the conclusion that internally manager portfolios can be more cheaply run. Why?

Ownership Mentality

The internal portfolio manager is an owner or an employee of the owner and in neither case has any need to hire a salesman to hawk the services of his department. Anyone who has received the extremely courteous self-service of a discount house knows firsthand how things can be cheaper without the overhead costs of sales personnel.

The entertainment budget for the investment department would conceivably be zero which, depending on one's point of view, might be interpreted as a plus or a minus. Not only does the department have no marketing costs, it also has no share of profit going to the owners of the

---

[10]Iain Jenkens, "Who Really Needs an Outside Manager, Anyway?" *Global Finance* (October 1996): 13-16.

[11]Calpers May Bring More Assets In-House," *Pensions & Investments* (March 3, 1997): 1, 44.

external manager or, in the case of a single outside manager, his share of profits. One could argue that the direct and variable costs of the internal department are parallel to the outside manager's profit margin. But it is postulated here that even under such a matchup the internal costs could be bare-boned compared with most of the higher profit margins of America's larger investment advice providers.

Compound Interest If the case is made that internal management is more cost-effective, to that extent must be added the effect of compounding. Even the smallest savings, if a regularly occurring benefit, will grow to substantial numbers when viewed in the context of a long-term pension, endowment, or other asset group. The compound effect might be much enlarged in those cases where outside performance fees and management contracts call for escalating shares of profits or flow-through of operating or other expense, such as with limited partnerships or real estate syndicates.

Direct Control of Sponsor

One intangible advantage of internal management — directly within the experience of this writer — can best be described by citing occurrences under the two modes of management, internal and external. When his sponsor organization was managing the portfolio, the purchase of an illegal or prohibited security was virtually unheard of.

In one case, a single security of a Canadian *corporate* bond was purchased under an authority to own Canadian *government* bonds. The trade was caught immediately in the internal audit system and reversed with no cost to the portfolio.

Later, when an outside manager was hired and given legal and otherwise limited security lists, that outside manager ignored the restrictions while purchasing a list of "illegal" holdings — with subsequent liquidation under unfavorable market conditions.

It should be stated that this type of comparison may not be as telling as more systems drop arbitrary restrictions completely and adopt the prudent-man rule. Even though the prudent-man rule may reign supreme in most areas, many may wonder when and if tobacco securities may be forcibly ejected from portfolios, as other "sin" holdings were dumped in the past and are still tacitly avoided today.[12]

---

[12]See *Pension & Investments* daily fax service, "P & I Daily" (July 2, 1997): 1, which reports the Pennsylvania Public School Employees instructing their money managers to stop buying tobacco stocks.

Interaction Fiduciaries with extensive portfolios will find that running assets in-house has the effect of improving knowledge and facility of interaction with any external managers that may be used. It can be compared to the officer who is actually on the front line with his troops. He knows firsthand what the terrain is, the intensity of enemy fire, and other aspects unavailable to rear guard brass.

In-House Specialists A moment should be given to the availability of in-house specialists. In 1975 there were approximately 4,200 Chartered Financial Analysts in America. Today there are over 20,000 CFAs and over 26,000 enrolled as AIMR (Association for Investment Management and Research) members all over the world. Some of the newer managers have not practiced through a serious market decline, so the number of seasoned advisers may be somewhat more limited than the number of CFA or AIMR certificates would indicate. Suffice it to say, the supply of investment professionals is adequate. An interesting possibility lies in hiring talented managers away from external systems. This usually will take the form of a clique of seasoned managers leaving one firm en masse to form another that eventually serves the same sponsors. This is not quite the same as making them employees of the sponsor, but is more prevalent than simple employment by the external manager client.

Another observation may be apropos here, again based on professional experience. When operating with one balanced manager, with an in-house liaison, this writer noted that all investment staff were immediately available to all members of the sponsor organization. After switching to a multiple manager/consultant format, communication changed to a strictly call-back mode with the call back often coming not in hours but days.

LEGAL RAMIFICATIONS

Some pension attorneys will point to some legal buffer afforded by outside management, although they will insist that the outside manager carry errors-and-omission insurance. The rationale is that by making the outside manager a fiduciary, as is done in external management contracts, the trustee "owner" reduces possible liability for his actions as long as he can show due process and due diligence — not in investment decisions, but in the selection and retention of outside managers.

Those public pension plans that use both internal and external management know that the total return for the plan is ultimately the responsibility of the trustees. They are the ones who will be elected or appointed for the record they establish.

It is submitted here that governing boards are equally responsible for their stewardship, whatever the mode of operation they choose, internal, external, or otherwise.

Team Effort

There remain some important advantages of outside management. One is true team effort. In some cases of internal management, especially in fixed-income management, the job may ostensibly be a team effort utilizing analysts, portfolio manager, trader, back office, economist, sector expert, etc. In actual practice, the job devolves to one in-house person. In this case, we still have an internal decision; but when it occurs, the trustee-fiduciary should know who is making it.

Additionally, mention should be made of the dilutive effect of in-house people who usually will have other jobs to do beside the money management function. Another interesting problem for internal modes is the question of what the fiduciary can do when the internal manager recommends that internal functions or part of them be hired out to an external manager? Would this be tantamount to quitting?

Coping with Flops

Another advantage of external management stems from the question: What do you do if your in-house managers flop? Regular employees are difficult to fire. With some civil service public employees, it may be a practical impossibility. The only solution to ending a bad string of performance could be to promote the manager to a nondiscretionary slot — as a damage-control device.

In some cases, performance contracts or bonuses are prevented by the very civil service codes insuring tenure, so no monetary incentives are possible. Performance contracts could be used in some cases but, then, most investment horizons extend to full market cycles — which also might make for long and attenuated time periods between possible corrective actions.

Debate continues as to when these "market cycles" occur and how long they last. In any case, anyone agreeing to performance employment might take on the trappings of an external manager and might find incentive to include profit margins and sales costs in his or her compensation. Be that as it may, common sense would indicate that an outside manager is a lot easier to switch than a full internal staff. On the other hand, the external manager also may not be easy to fire due to political pressures, habit, individual trustee alliances, etc.

The Rotation Phenomenon In this vein should be mentioned the phenomenon of industry rotation of professional managers. There are endless searches on the adviser business. A glance at any industry trade paper shows the meticulous listing of new searches, searches in progress, completed searches, planned searches, ideas of plans of searches, and rumors. If the trustee's maintenance and care of outside managers is viewed from an industrywide perspective, the whole process may be defined not as the hiring and firing of managers, but as the camouflaged swapping and rotation of these managers between sponsors. As one deselected manager aptly described this phenomenon, "We are not out of your game, we're just on the bench for awhile."

Who's Calling the Shots?

Let's continue this simile in light of the concentration of assets in the larger consultant firms. Does the consultant referee the game as well as do all the play assignments and substitutions? Are the sponsor owners kept on the sidelines? Does this team strategy obviate to some degree the apparent hiring, monitoring, and firing of the managers in the adviser community? This possibility would certainly be worthy of further research.

The performance of all portfolios of all the active managers in the market must add up to the performance of the total market. The average performer in this milieu underperforms the market return earned by indexed investors by the cost of pursuing active management activities. Any plan fiduciary using active managers must be sure to have a reliable process for picking, auditing, and firing managers, to employ only the ones who actually add value over the passive index. The collective choice of managers is far more valuable to overall plan results than the management ability of any individual manager.

THE BUCK STOPS AT THE BOARD

To most people who have a opportunity to apply the arguments presented here in a practical setting, a natural conclusion would be that — whether internal or external management is used — the ultimate responsibility lies with the governing board of a public pension fund.

At one time in the history of trust and asset management, it was argued that public entities should not be part of the more esoteric parts of the capital markets. This could be surmised from the very restrictive legal lists that possibly overemphasized capital preservation at the expense of optimum return. Some probate courts will not allow child estates to own anything but U. S. government bonds.

Public entities that were once viewed as outside the private sector were, therefore, counseled to look to a growth target not to exceed the real growth in the stock of capital goods in the national economy — what some economists call the average real return on capital. Any gains in excess of the real growth of capital might be considered trading gains, in the sense that any market gain must necessarily result in a loss to another player in the market. By logical extension, public entities were not supposed to try to beat the market averages, each other, or other managers. Their mission was simply to hold long-term assets and earn the most secure long-term rate of return consistent with maximum safety. Such a retrenched viewpoint will certainly have to wait for a serious correction to the bull market in American securities that is now part of the longest economic expansion in the nation's history.

MAKING MEANINGFUL COMPARISONS

The skills of the internal staff, the resources needed, the activities used by internal and external managers are arguably different.[13] The decision to manage internally or to go outside plays a role in the classic make-or-buy literature of accounting and decision-making.

Passive management (the kind typically conducted in-house) usually calls for commoditylike management in which control of costs is critical and, therefore, amenable to internal procedures. Active management is sought for its potential added value over passive performance; expense factors are involved in its pursuit. This favors external management. However, if product niches are carefully selected and crossover benefits of internal research are taken into account, targeted internal active equity management can be very competitive with external alternatives. Calpers, for example, currently manages passive portfolios — comprising primarily large-capitalization companies — internally. All active-equity and small-company passive portfolios are managed externally.

CONCLUSION

As more fiduciaries become expert in modern portfolio theory, we may see a drift to more internal management by large and midsize funds and trusts. This will remain a challenge to professional managers who hire out for fees, despite the fact that recently they have been faring very well in terms of market share.

---

[13]Calpers internal memo on investment strategies, 1997 (unpublished).

Garry M. Allen, CFA, is the founder, president and chief investment officer of Two Rivers Capital Management at Kingsmill, Inc. The firm specializes in investments for institutional equity and fixed income, as well as high-net-worth individuals.

Two Rivers is a registered investment advisory firm based in Colonial Williamsburg, Virginia, at the Busch Corporate Center.

Prior to creation of Two Rivers in August 1997, Allen was president and CIO of Virtus Capital Management, a wholly owned investment subsidiary of Signet Banking Corp. He served as managing director of U.S. equities at the Virginia Retirement System prior to joining Virtus Capital Management.

Allen holds a bachelor of science degree in in business from Virginia Tech and a master's degree in business administration from the College of William and Mary. He is also a Chartered Financial Analyst.

T. Daniel Coggin is the director of research for TeamVest, LLC an investment management consulting firm in Charlotte, NC. Coggin has 20 years of experience in investment management and consulting, and has a Ph.D. in political economy from Michigan State University.

Before joining TeamVest, he was director of research for the Virginia Retirement System (a $35 billion state retirement fund) and a visiting professor of applied finance at the University of North Carolina at Charlotte.

Coggin has authored and co-authored over 25 articles in leading finance and investment management journals. He has also contributed a number of chapters to edited investment management books and coedited three books on quantitative investment management.

In addition to his duties at TeamVest, Coggin serves on the editorial boards of the *Journal of Portfolio Management*, the *Journal of Investing*, and the *Review of Quantitative Finance and Accounting*.

Chapter 2

Organizing Internal Investment Management

Garry M. Allen, CFA
President and Chief Investment Officer
Two Rivers Capital Management at Kingsmill, Inc.

T. Daniel Coggin, Ph.D.
Director of Research
TeamVest, LLC

uch has been written about the characteristics of "successful" organizations. Indeed, entire college courses and even graduate degrees are offered in organizational behavior, organizational theory, and management. This chapter has a much more specific goal. In this chapter we provide a brief outline of an organizational structure for internal investment management. By internal investment management, we mean in-house investment units or groups charged with the task of investing all or part of the pension or investment fund of a corporation, governmental unit or foundation. We will refer to the sponsoring agent as the "sponsor" and to the investment fund as the "plan." To be sure, a number of important articles have been written on successful management of investment organizations. A monograph sponsored by the Institute of Chartered Financial Analysts was devoted to the subject.[1] This chapter seeks to contribute to this important literature by presenting what we believe is an innovative and flexible model of investment organizational structure.

There are two components of any organization (successful or unsuccessful): people (human resources) and structure. Both are critical to the successful organization. We readily agree that the human resource component is worthy of intense focus and study by the investment organization and its students. We dare say all investment organizations could benefit from more attention to such people-related activities as psycho-

---

[1] J. R. Vertin, ed., *Managing the Investment Organization* (Charlottesville, VA: The Institute of Chartered Financial Analysts, 1988).

logical testing, and employee training and development (e.g., sensitivity training, motivational training, etc.). However, that is not the focus of this chapter. This chapter will focus on the second component, the structure of the organization. We present an outline of an investment organizational structure that will allow the investment organization to deal with the challenges to successful internal investment management we foresee for the year 2000 and beyond.

The remainder of our chapter is divided into three major sections. The next section discusses the challenges to internal investment management. We follow with our model of an organizational structure to meet these challenges. The final section summarizes our presentation. While we focus here on internal equity management, our proposed model is applicable to investment management in general.

CHALLENGES TO INVESTMENT MANAGEMENT

It should be no surprise that the challenges to successful investment management in the late 1990s are essentially the same as those in the 1970s, the 1960s, or any other period. The perennial challenges to successful investment management include: investment performance, maintaining a consistent investment process, creativity, organizational turnover, and employee compensation.

Investment performance was placed first on the list of challenges for a specific reason. The cold hard fact of the investment profession is that, in the final analysis, performance is the most important factor. In the case of the internal asset manager, the specific investment objective is supplied by the plan sponsor. Whether the investment objective is to outperform the S&P 500 Stock Index (S&P 500) or some "normal portfolio,"[2] it must eventually be achieved if the investment management effort is to be deemed successful. An investment industry rule of thumb is three to five years and an outside manager is "up or out." While some sponsors have an even shorter time horizon, very few have a longer time horizon.

There is increasing evidence that the majority of active equity managers do not outperform the stock market (defined as the S&P 500).[3]

---

[2]The normal portfolio is fully discussed in J.A. Christopherson, "Normal Portfolios and Their Construction," Chapter 17 in F. J. Fabozzi, ed., *Active Equity Portfolio Management* (New Hope, PA: Frank J. Fabozzi Associates, 1998).

[3]For evidence on this point, see T.D. Coggin, "Active Equity Management," Chapter 4 in *Portfolio & Investment Management*; A.S. Wood, "Fatal Attractions for Money Managers" (Chicago, IL: Probus Publishing Co., 1989), *Financial Analysts Journal* 45 (May/June 1989), pp. 3-5; and M. Siconolfi, "More Stock Mutual Funds Fall Behind in Crowded Race," *The Wall Street Journal*, October 13, 1989.

Some have viewed this as evidence that active equity management is a "loser's game" and that it is therefore fruitless (and even hypocritical) to attempt it. The organizational model presented here does not make such an assumption. In fact, our model is neutral on the issue. It can accommodate both active and passive investment styles. Our model does, however, make some assumptions about human judgment.

The noted investment consultant Richard Ennis was quoted as saying:

> Many of the best money managers are almost completely intuitive. You can use a computer to price certain standard instruments like options. But your best chance of beating the market by a meaningful margin is with *people of uncommon ability who observe subtleties, make judgments and weigh thousands of facts and observations in a powerful, analytical and intuitive way* (emphasis added).[4]

Ennis is quite confident of this opinion. Unfortunately, it is not supported by the evidence on the issue. Studies of human judgment consistently show that it is prone to errors and biases resulting from the selected overuse of information of limited and/or questionable validity.[5] Other studies consistently show that well-formulated statistical models outperform even trained professionals in making judgments.[6]

Other studies have shown that a majority of investment managers do not use quantitative methods to value common stocks. A survey reported in *Pensions & Investment Age* (November 10, 1986) reported that only 8% of respondents use quantitative methods to manage stocks; and a survey conducted by Arthur D. Little, Inc. in March 1987 reported that only 30% of respondents indicated intensive use of quantitative methods in their overall money management effort. This small minority of quantitative managers spans a continuum from using analysts to provide input to quantitative models to using *no* analysts at all, relying

---

[4]"Richard Ennis on Getting Manager's Best Shots," *Pensions & Investment Age*, October 2, 1989, 62.

[5]For a good introduction to this literature, see D. Kahneman, P. Slovic, and A. Tversky, eds., *Judgment Under Uncertainty: Heuristics and Biases* (New York, NY: Cambridge University Press, 1982).

[6]The classic study is P. E. Meehl, *Clinical Versus Statistical Prediction* (Minneapolis, MN: University of Minnesota Press, 1954). Meehl's basic finding has since been supported by numerous studies in several different fields.

instead on computers and "artificial intelligence" to process information, select and trade stocks.[7] Hence, 30 years after the "quantitative revolution" of the late 1960s, most money managers apparently continue to rely on conventional (i.e., nonquantitative) methods of investment management. In the case of stocks, this generally means that financial analysts perform fundamental security analysis and make recommendations to portfolio managers about which stocks to buy and sell. A relatively large *subjective component* is then applied to the final investment decision. No doubt, this process has been successful for some investment managers. However, it is our opinion that an increasing number of investment organizations will be forced by the pressure of underperformance to explore the use of quantitative investment models and techniques.

Maintaining a consistent investment process is high on the list of characteristics of successful investment organizations. Any investment management consultant will verify that one of the first things to look for in evaluating an investment organization is a consistent and well-defined investment process. *Creativity* is also crucial. The investment organization's ability to adapt to the ever-changing market environment with new and innovative ideas is a major challenge. *Organizational turnover* is another variable high on the management consultant's list. The bane of sponsors is the all-too-frequent "here today, gone tomorrow" nature of investment management professionals. Last but not least, *employee compensation* is a key challenge to investment management. The ability to effectively link compensation to organizational goals and productivity is often lacking in investment organizations. The problem is especially critical in organizations characterized by the "star system." One or two key investment "stars" command high salaries while the "supporting cast" is significantly underpaid on a relative basis. Even so, the stars often move to another firm, tempted by an even higher salary

The next section outlines an organizational structure that addresses each of these challenges. Our proposed structure is characterized by a quantitative, model-driven approach to investment management. In view of the facts and challenges listed above, we view our model as the "shape of things to come" in the ongoing evolution of investment organizational structure.

---

[7]As a case in point, see the article on Rosenberg Institutional Equity Management, "Inside the Alpha Factory," *Institutional Investor*, September 1989, pp. 141-145.

THE VALUE CHAIN
ORGANIZATIONAL STRUCTURE

In the typical investment group, too little time is spent thinking about organizational structure. Most investment units are structured along the lines of the traditional, hierarchical pyramid organization model. Historically, the traditional pyramid is best applied in mechanistic, hierarchical, or bureaucratic organizations. In an established bureaucracy, with clear rules and operating procedures and chains of command, the static pyramid structure has a natural environment. Pyramids have survived because they are frequently applied in situations characterized by limited competition, simple environments, and predictable relationships. However, in the most *competitive* arenas of business enterprise (such as the investment arena), the traditional pyramid structure is not withstanding the test of time. The pyramid is today being challenged by such well-known management consultants as Ken Blanchard, who believes the pyramid should be turned upside down, with the customer (in our case, the sponsor) as the focal point of attention.[8] Peters and Waterman's now classic book, *In Search of Excellence* (1982), also emphasizes this basic point.

The investment world is characterized by high levels of uncertainty, complexity and nonroutine technologies. It lacks those static and predictable relationships found in traditional pyramid organizations. A wealth of real-time information must be effectively managed and quickly turned into usable investment knowledge. Investment units must, therefore, have a fluid organizational structure. That is, a form that is adaptive, flexible, and capable of managing information with a fast response time. More specifically, a structure that can quickly turn opportunity into knowledge, knowledge into action, and action into performance for the plan.

While the traditional pyramid allows a hierarchy of responsibility, talent, or even ego, rarely has it addressed the issues of strategy and competitive advantage. Our challenge is to apply creativity at the *organizational structure* level, not just at the investment process or product level. There is a revolution going on in the thought process of organizational design. The organization that sits back and holds on to mechanistic and bureaucratic form and symbolism will not survive in the investment arena.We believe that successful investment groups are already integrating form and function, and that pyramids will not be the structure of choice in the late 1990s and beyond.

One of the basic principles of business policy is that strategy determines structure. At the core of strategic thinking is the pursuit of

---

[8]K. Blanchard and S. Johnson, *The One Minute Manager* (New York, NY: William Morrow, 1982).

competitive advantage. We believe that competitive advantage can be built into organizational structure, just as competitive advantage has been built into the product level. There exists a tremendous gap between traditional organizational structures that resemble pyramids and the functioning of the organization as defined through job descriptions. In reality, the two can be linked in a manner that creates *sustainable* competitive advantage.

The Value Chain

The value chain concepts set forth by Michael E. Porter in his book on competitive business strategy[9] can be applied to organizational structure in ways that directly link human resource management with the economic value of the firm. The result is a *functional* organization structure for investment management; a structure that flattens the pyramid and aligns form, function, responsibility, and accountability into a single dimension. That is, a structure that strikes at the heart of the key investment challenges of today and the future: performance, process, creativity, people, and compensation. Too often today's organizational structures pull apart critical success factors and never successfully reconnect them into a cohesive organization with competitive advantage. We believe the following value chain organizational structure provides a platform for managing a fluid investment organization.

The organizational premises behind the value chain structure are:

1. *Level the organizational structure.* Flatten the traditional pyramid into a form that symbolizes the fluid and dynamic character of investment management. A form that is dynamic, responsive and solution-driven fosters creativity and is results-oriented. Expect talented individuals to add value every day. Quantify and link performance with responsibility and accountability. The stock market chalks up gains and losses every day; the people that invest in it should know if their investment effort helped or hurt the plan in the short run. The sponsor will know quickly enough! While short-run investment performance can be (and often is) *overemphasized*, reasonable attention to timely achievement of specified goals is highly desirable.

2. *Rebuild the structure around functional components.* At the conceptual level, the investment unit performs research & development, production, and monitoring. Our proposed structure

---

[9]M. E. Porter, *Competitive Advantage* (New York, NY: The Free Press, 1985).

should provide answers to such key questions and issues as: Should we build a new investment model? (Research Team); *Can* we build the model? (Systems Development and Data Management); *Build* the model (Production Systems Group); *Execute* the model (Trading); and *Monitor* the model (Investment Administration). The structure presented here provides *feedback loops* between the operating components so that no subunit is working in isolation, and the appropriate interchanges occur between them. There is a principle of continuous interdependence in place, while clear operating boundaries define lines of accountability. Our proposed structure is diagrammed in Exhibit 1.

In our structure, the essential functions are carried out by organizational subunits called *teams*:

Component	*Function*
Research Team	Ideas & Issues
Systems Development & Data Management	Database & Data Management
Portfolio Systems Team	Model-Building
Trading	Execution
Investment Administration & Performance Measurement	Monitor Process & Results

The Research Team is the primary forum for brainstorming, idea generation, and debating issues. The discussion of why a model should be built or enhanced occurs at this level. Once a decision is made to move forward with a model, the Systems Development & Data Management (SDDM) team obtains the necessary building blocks of data needed to construct the model. The SDDM team must turn the critical data over to the Portfolio Systems Team (PST) in a format readily usable by quantitative model builders. That is, the data should be structured and formatted by SDDM into the research format used by the PST. For example, SDDM would convert financial data (from COMPUSTAT) and expectational data (from IBES) into a relational database such as INGRES, which is them used by the PST.

The PST performs the model-building and quantitative task. This team transforms concepts into a real-world, operational investment model. Backtesting is performed to increase confidence in the model. Once built and tested, the model is launched via trading *execution*, and closely *monitored* by Investment Administration. The teams have been

Exhibit 1: Investment Organizational Structure

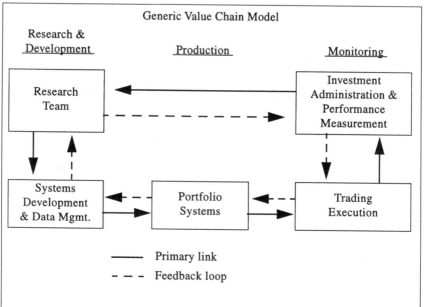

aligned in a value chain such that the previous tasks must be completed before the next group can add its value. Any weaknesses in the links will surface quickly via the monitoring and control process, and feedback.

3. *Redefine team portfolio management.* Team portfolio management is not the traditional investment management-by-committee process. In many cases, the management-by-committee approach has failed due to "groupthink" or the consensus instinct to "follow the herd."[10]

An integral part of our team management structure is the concept of "designated experts." These designated experts handle assigned issues, areas of responsibility, and specific models. They act as *team leaders* of groups assigned to address specific topics and problems. The designated expert has ultimate responsibility for success or failure in the assigned area. This approach develops great depth and cross-training as different "special teams take the field" for different sets of challenges.

---

[10]For a good discussion of this problem and the advantages of the model portfolio/team approach to investment management, see D. J. Forrestal, III "Control of the Investment Management Process Within the Large Organization," in J.R. Vertin, ed., *Managing the Investment Organization.*

BENEFITS TO THE VALUE CHAIN ORGANIZATIONAL STRUCTURE

The following set of benefits can be directly attributed to using the value chain investment organizational structure:

1. *Embeds competitive advantage into the core of the investment management structure.* When form, functionality, and accountability are creatively linked into a single investment system encompassing structure and process, the investment unit is operating at its maximum capacity for response to opportunity and crisis. To illustrate the benefits to timely analysis and appropriate response, some investment groups correctly assessed the 508-point DJIA plunge to 1738 on October 19, 1987, as an opportunity rather than a crash. With that assessment, those groups began buying stocks the following week and rejoicing as the DJIA recovered and rose to 9328 on July 16, 1998. Crisis and opportunity always stand side by side, framed by uncertainty and disguised with complexity. The highest reward will go to the investment unit that can quickly and correctly unravel events, isolate causal factors, and position itself accordingly. An organization can respond only as quickly as its structure will allow it to respond.

2. *Provides a model for engineered solutions to investment problems.* The investment world is evolving toward "structured" asset management. We believe that the structured investment process will gradually supplant the *ad hoc* approaches of the past. Engineered solutions to investment management involve decision rules based upon quantitative investment models. Engineered solutions serve to raise the information content of the investment processes to the highest level attainable. An engineered solution may stand alone or form the basis for an investment process which allows more human intervention.

3. *Problems will surface more quickly, enabling management to be proactive rather than reactive.* It would be enough if our structure only satisfied needs derived from investment-related demands. However, the structure is equally adept at flushing out problem situations in the human resource management area. The flattened organizational structure allows attitudes and egos not conducive to team-building to surface and become visible more quickly than traditional pyramid structures. Management can

then move to resolve issues before they become more serious.

4. *Insulates the investment unit from damaging turnover of key personnel with the team approach.* Professional turnover is a fact of life in the world of investment management. The investment unit requires stability of the investment process *independent* of key personnel turnover. Units with purely judgmental decision-makers and/or poorly structured processes are extremely vulnerable to the departure of key figures. A specific function or the *entire* unit may be placed in jeopardy because of turnover in key positions. While nothing can completely absorb the impact of a key person departing, the team portfolio management approach helps insulate the investment process from the damaging effects of key departures.

5. *Links strategy, accountability, and compensation into a single organizational structure.* The bureaucratic pyramid investment organization fights against atrophy, malaise, and inertia as much as it battles the stock market. The organization's response time is slowed by layer upon layer of procedures and rules. Few have final responsibility or can act alone. This is not an organizational structure designed for investment performance. Entrepreneurism and risk-taking have long departed this organizational climate. Our structure serves to streamline strategy, process, and accountability, as well as monitor the contributions of individuals.

6. *Develops depth and cross-training of skills.* Special teams headed by designated experts add natural depth and training to the organization and ensure that all essential skills are well covered. While there is sufficient room for individual creativity and growth, no one works in isolation; and the integration of form and function helps to provide continuity.

7. *The "star" is the system rather than the individual.* A prime example of this approach to investment management is Rosenberg Institutional Equity Management (RIEM) in Orinda, California. At RIEM, there are no stars, only team members. As if to emphasize the completely quantitative nature of the process, those who monitor portfolios are called "portfolio engineers."

8. *Makes it easier to match the right talent to the right position in the organization, since areas of expertise are well-defined.* Often

in a purely generalist environment, it can be hard to determine who is adding value and who is along for the ride. Our structure recognizes the need to leverage special skills and talents, and yet maintain some boundaries of responsibility.

9. *Allows the investment unit to focus on who the competition really is — the S&P 500 or an appropriate benchmark, not each other.* In our system, performance comes first. The team is united in the belief that the opposition is the benchmark, and not other teammates. Rewards are based on team accomplishments as well as individual achievement.

10. *Requires interaction, which is the key to effective teamwork.* The value chain structure requires continuous interaction: first, through the natural progression of building value and second, through the feedback loop for reciprocal communication. Complex tasks can be segmented and apportioned based on specialized skills, and then brought back together for an overall evaluation.

CONCLUSION

This chapter has assumed an ambitious task — to provide a model of internal investment organizational structure for the 1990s and beyond. We see the investment management profession at a crossroads. The challenges of performance, consistency, creativity, turnover, and compensation are now perhaps more pressing and intense than at any other point in the history of the profession. We do not believe that the traditional, static pyramid organizational structure will survive in this environment.

We have presented a flexible and dynamic organizational structure based upon the value chain principle elaborated by Michael Porter.[11] Our proposed structure is built around functional components headed by "team leaders" and "designated experts" who are responsible for the success or failure of each specific assignment. This structure embeds competitive advantage into the core of the management structure and provides a framework for engineered solutions to investment problems and challenges.

---

[11]See also I. Schmerken, "CIOs Orchestrate Trading, Teamwork As New Portfolio Analysis Theme," *Wall Street Computer Review*, November 1989.

Bruce I. Jacobs is a principal of Jacobs Levy Equity Management, Roseland, N. J. Founded in 1986, Jacobs Levy focuses exclusively on active management of U.S. equity portfolios, based on the firm's proprietary methods of disentangling the market's complex web of profit opportunities. The firm currently manages $5 billion in institutional assets.

Before founding Jacobs Levy with co-principal Kenneth N. Levy, Jacobs was senior managing director of a quantitative equity management affiliate of the Prudential Asset Management Co. He is currently on the advisory board of the *Journal of Portfolio Management*. His book, *Capital Ideas and Market Realities*, will be published in 1999.

Jacobs holds a B.A. from Columbia College, an M.S. in operations research and computer science from Columbia University's School of Engineering and Applied Science, an M.S.I.A. from Carnegie-Mellon, and an M.A. in applied economics and a Ph.D. in finance from the University of Pennsylvania's Wharton School.

Kenneth N. Levy is a principal of Jacobs Levy Equity Management. He was formerly managing director of a quantitative equity management affiliate of the Prudential Asset Management Co. He has served on the advisory board of POSIT and the CFA curriculum committee.

Levy's articles with Jacobs have appeared in the *Financial Analysts Journal*, the *Journal of Portfolio Management*, the *Journal of Investing*, and the *Japanese Security Analysts Journal*. Their article, "Disentangling Equity Return Regularities," received the AIMR's Graham and Dodd award.

Levy received a B.A. in economics from Cornell University and an M.B.A. and M.A. in applied economics from the Wharton School. He has completed all course requirements for his Ph.D. in finance at Wharton.

The authors thank Judith Kimball for her editorial assistance.

Chapter 3

Active Equity Management for Pension Plans

Bruce I. Jacobs, Ph.D.
Principal
Jacobs Levy Equity Management

Kenneth N. Levy, CFA
Principal
Jacobs Levy Equity Management

A pension plan that chooses an active equity manager expects to benefit from returns in excess of those achieved by a comparable passive manager. Whether those expectations will be met depends on how well the manager does at two basic related tasks. The first task is to detect mispriced securities. Mispriced securities have the potential to provide superior returns as their prices correct, over time, to fair values. The second task is to combine those securities in portfolios that preserve the superior returns without adding undue risk.

Sounds easy enough. Of course, it isn't. In fact, the efficient market hypothesis and random walk theory would say that it's impossible, that mispricing, if it existed at all, would be so fleeting or so random as to defy detection. And both research and reality have shown that simple selection rules, such as low price/earnings ratios, or even elegant, Ivory Tower theories such as the Capital Asset Pricing Model and Arbitrage Pricing Theory, are inadequate to the task.

Stock price behavior defies any simple analyses.[1] With the right research tools and enough perseverance, however, one can detect a complex web of interrelated return effects that form predictable patterns of mispricing across stocks and over time. These patterns may be exploited for superior performance.

The equity market is what scientists would call a complex system. Random systems, such as Brownian motion and white noise (static), are the product of a large number of variables, cannot be modeled, and

---

[1]See, for example, Bruce I. Jacobs and Kenneth N. Levy, "The Complexity of the Stock Market," *Journal of Portfolio Management* (Fall 1989).

are inherently unpredictable. Ordered systems, such as the structure of diamond crystals or the dynamics of pendulums, are definable by a relatively small number of variables and predictable by relatively simple rules. Complex systems, such as the weather and the workings of DNA, can be at least partly comprehended and modeled, but only with great difficulty. The number of variables that must be modeled, and their interactions, are beyond the capacity of the human mind alone. Only with the aid of advanced computational science can the mysteries of complex systems be unraveled.[2]

A complex market, that is, requires a complex selection model. This chapter describes one such model. It also discusses how such a model can be implemented so as to maximize return and minimize risk for a wide variety of investment goals. We begin with the very basic question of how a manager should approach the equity market. Should he or she attempt to cover the broadest possible range of stocks, or can greater analytical insights be garnered by focusing on a particular subset of the market or a limited number of stocks?

TAKING A BROAD APPROACH

Investment managers have traditionally followed several distinct approaches to stock selection. Value managers, for example, have concentrated on buying stocks selling at prices perceived to be low relative to the company's assets or earnings. Growth managers have sought stocks with above-average earnings growth not fully reflected in price. Small-capitalization managers have looked for opportunity in stocks that have been overlooked by most investors.

The valuation approaches of investment managers have left their tracks on the behavior of the stocks comprising the selection pool. Most prominent is the tendency for stocks to subdivide into distinct style segments — into growth and value, large- and small-cap groupings. Client preferences have encouraged this Balkanization of the market, and the actions of investment consultants have formalized it.

Consultants have designed style indexes and have defined managers in terms of their proclivity for one style or another. Managers may thus find a particular style orientation effectively imposed on them. To the extent that a manager's performance is measured against a given style index, deviations from the index give rise to added investment and business risk. Consequently, a manager may find it advantageous to stick

---

[2]See, for example, Heinz Pagels, *The Dreams of Reason: The Computer and the Rise of the Sciences of Complexity* (New York, NY: Simon and Schuster, 1988).

closely to a given style.

An investment approach that focuses on individual market segments can have its advantages. Such an approach recognizes, for example, that the U.S. equity market is neither entirely homogeneous nor entirely heterogeneous. All stocks do not react alike to a given impetus, nor does each stock exhibit its own, totally idiosyncratic price behavior. Rather, stocks within a given style, or sector, or industry tend to behave similarly to each other and somewhat differently from stocks outside their group.

While style preferences and other forces act to segment the equity market, however, other forces act to integrate it. After all, there exist some managers who select their portfolios from the broad universe of stocks, and others who, while they may focus on a particular type of stock given current economic conditions, are poised to change their focus should underlying conditions change. The capital of these investors flows across style segments, integrating the overall market.

Most importantly, all stocks can be defined by the same fundamental parameters — by market capitalization, price/earnings ratio, dividend discount model ranking, and so on. All stocks can be found at some level on the continuum of values for each parameter. Growth and value stocks inhabit the opposite ends of the continua of P/E and dividend yield, and small and large stocks the opposite ends of the continua of firm capitalization and analyst coverage. Moreover, these positions are not static. An out-of-favor growth stock may slip into value territory. A small-cap company may grow into the large-cap range.

Arbitrage works toward market integration. If too many investors want low P/E, for example, low-P/E stocks will be bid up to higher P/E levels. Some investors will step in to sell them and buy other stocks deserving of higher P/Es. An investment approach that focuses on the individual segments of the market ignores the powerful forces that work to integrate, rather than segment, the market.

The market's tenuous balance between integration and segmentation is one dimension of its complexity. This dimension calls for an investment approach that is 180 degrees removed from the narrow, segment-oriented focus of traditional management. It requires an approach that takes into account the behavior of stocks across the broadest possible selection universe, without losing sight of the significant differences in price behavior that distinguish particular market segments.

Almost by default, this twin task demands a quantitative approach. Quantitative tools have the capacity to handle the widest selection universe and, at the same time, the capability of going into great depth and detail of analysis. To the same myriad fundamental and economic data used in traditional security valuation, quantitative analysis can apply modern computing power, finance theory and statistical techniques that extend the reaches (and discipline the vagaries) of the human mind.

Starting off with the broadest possible view of the equity selection universe allows the investment manager to approach the investment problem with an unbiased philosophy. The manager can then choose to use a more narrowly defined focal point from which to frame the market. But beginning with the wider-angle lens ensures that the manager's investment approach has two important qualities — coherence and completeness.

Coherence and Completeness

To the extent that the market is integrated, an investment approach that models each industry or style segment as if it were a universe unto itself is not the best approach. Consider, for example, a firm that offers both core and value strategies. Suppose the firm runs a model on its total universe of, say, 3,000 stocks. It then runs the same model or a different, segment-specific model on a 500-stock subset of large-cap value stocks.

If different models are used for each strategy, the results will differ. Even if the same model is estimated separately for each strategy, its results will differ because the model coefficients are bound to differ between the broader universe and the narrower segment. What if the core model predicts GM will outperform Ford, while the value model shows the reverse? Should the investor start the day with multiple estimates of one stock's alpha? This would violate what we call the "Law of One Alpha."[3]

Of course, the firm could ensure coherence by using separate models for each market segment — growth, value, small-cap — and linking the results via a single, overarching model that relates all the subsets. But the firm then runs into a second problem with segmented investment approaches: To the extent that the market is integrated, the pricing of securities in one segment may contain information relevant to pricing in other segments. But the interrelationships between stocks and stock subsets become clear only when viewed from the perspective of the whole.

For example, within a generally well integrated national economy, labor market conditions in the United States differ region by region. An economist attempting to model employment in the Northeast would

---

[3]See Bruce I. Jacobs and Kenneth N. Levy, "The Law of One Alpha," *Journal of Portfolio Management* (Summer 1995).

probably consider economic expansion in the Southeast. Similarly, the investor who wants to model growth stocks should not ignore value stocks. The effects of inflation, say, on value stocks may have repercussions for growth stocks; after all, the two segments represent opposite ends of the same P/E continuum.

An investment approach that concentrates on a single market segment does not make use of all available information. A wide-angle approach considers all the stocks in the universe — value and growth, large- and small-cap. It benefits from all the information to be gleaned from a wide and diverse range of stock price behavior. It is thus poised to take advantage of more profit opportunities than a more narrowly focused approach affords.

Not Forgetting Depth

Breadth of inquiry must not come at the sacrifice of depth of inquiry. A complex security selection model does not ignore the significant differences across different types of stock, differences exploitable by specialized investing. What's more, in examining similarities and differences across market segments, it considers numerous variables that may be defining.

For value, say, a complex model does not confine itself to a dividend discount model measure of value, but also examines earnings, cash flow, sales, and yield value, among other attributes. Growth measurements to be considered include historical, expected, and sustainable growth, as well as the momentum and stability of earnings. Share price, volatility, and analyst coverage are among the elements to be considered along with market capitalization as measures of size.[4]

These variables are often closely correlated with each other. Small-cap stocks, for example, tend to have low P/Es; low P/E is correlated with high yield; both low P/E and high yield are correlated with

---

[4]At a deeper level of complexity, one must also consider alternative ways of specifying such fundamental variables as earnings or cash flow. Over what period does one measure earnings, for example? If using analyst earnings expectations, which measure provides the best estimate of future real earnings? The consensus of all available estimates made over the past six months? Only the very latest earnings estimates? Are some analysts more accurate or more influential? What if a recent estimate is not available for a given company? See Bruce I. Jacobs, Kenneth N. Levy, and Mitchell C. Krask, "Earnings Estimates, Predictor Specification, and Measurement Error," *Journal of Investing* (Summer 1997), pp. 29-46.

DDM estimates of value. Furthermore, they may be correlated with a stock's industry affiliation. A simple low-P/E screen, for example, will tend to select a large number of bank and utility stocks. Such correlations can distort naive attempts to relate returns to potentially relevant variables. A true picture of the variable-return relationship emerges only after "disentangling" the variables.

DISENTANGLING RETURNS

The effects of different sources of stock return can overlap. In Exhibit 1, the lines represent connections documented by academic studies; they may appear like a ball of yarn after the cat got to it. To unravel the connections between variables and return, it is necessary to examine all the variables simultaneously.

Exhibit 1: Return Effects Form a Tangled Web

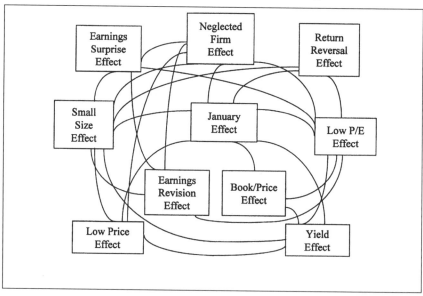

For instance, the low-P/E effect is widely recognized, as is the small-size effect. But stocks with low P/Es also tend to be of small size. Are P/E and size merely two ways of looking at the same effect? Or does each variable matter? Perhaps the excess returns to small-cap stocks are merely a January effect, reflecting the tendency of taxable investors to sell depressed stocks at year-end. Answering these questions requires disentangling return effects via multivariate regression.[5]

Common methods of measuring return effects, such as quintiling or univariate (single-variable) regression, are "naive" because they assume, naively, that prices are responding only to the single variable under consideration — low P/E, say. But a number of related variables may be affecting returns. As we have noted, small-cap stocks and banking and utility industry stocks tend to have low P/Es. A univariate regression of return on low P/E will capture, along with the effect of P/E, a great deal of "noise" related to firm size, industry affiliation, and other variables.

Simultaneous analysis of all relevant variables via multivariate regression takes into account and adjusts for such interrelationships. The result is the return to each variable separately, controlling for all related variables. A multivariate analysis for low P/E, for example, will provide a measure of the excess return to a portfolio that is market-like in all respects except for a single distinguishing feature — a lower-than-average P/E ratio. Disentangled returns are "pure" returns.

Noise Reduction

Exhibit 2 plots naive and pure cumulative excess (relative to a 3,000-stock universe) returns to high book-to-price ratio.[6] The naive returns show a great deal of volatility; the pure returns, by contrast, follow a much smoother path. There is a lot of noise in the naive returns. What causes it?

Note the divergence between the naive and pure return series for the 12 months starting in March 1979. This date coincides with the crisis at the nuclear power plant at Three Mile Island. Utilities such as GPU, operator of the Three Mile Island power plant, tend to have high B/Ps, and naive B/P measures will reflect the performance of these utilities along with the performance of other high-B/P stocks. Electric utility prices plummeted 24% after the Three Mile Island crisis. The naive B/P measure reflects this decline.

But industry-related events such as Three Mile Island have no necessary bearing on the book/price variable. An investor could, for

---

[5]See Bruce I. Jacobs and Kenneth N. Levy, "Disentangling Equity Return Regularities: New Insights and Investment Opportunities," *Financial Analysts Journal* (May/June 1988).

[6]In particular, naive and pure returns are provided by a portfolio having a book-to-price ratio that is one standard deviation above the universe mean book-to-price ratio. For pure returns, the portfolio is also constrained to have universe-average exposures to all the other variables in the model, including fundamental characteristics and industry affiliations.

example, hold a high-B/P portfolio that does not overweight utilities, and such a portfolio would not have experienced the decline reflected in the naive B/P measure in Exhibit 2. The naive returns to B/P reflect noise from the inclusion of a utility industry effect. A pure B/P measure is not contaminated by such irrelevant variables.

Exhibit 2: Naive and Pure Returns to High Book-to-Price Ratio

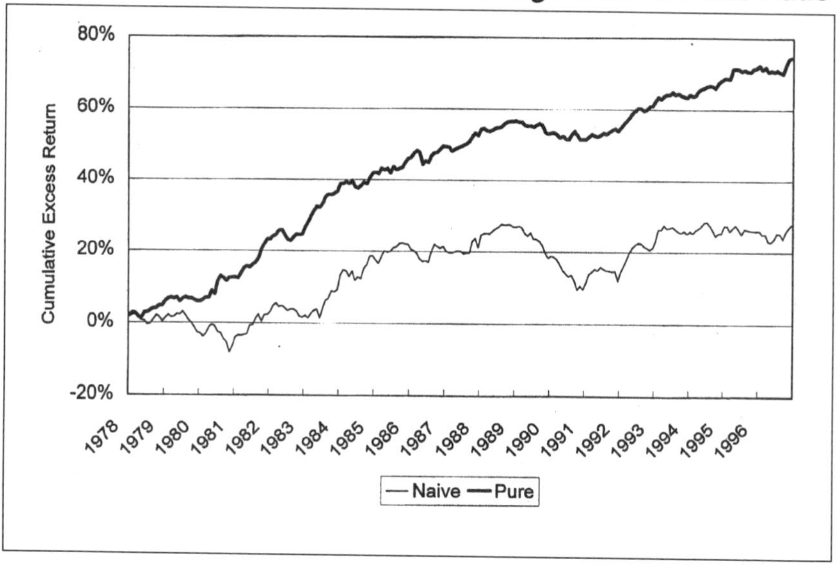

Disentangling distinguishes real effects from mere proxies and thereby distinguishes between real and spurious investment opportunities. As it separates high B/P and industry affiliation, for example, it can also separate the effects of firm size from the effects of related variables. Disentangling shows that returns to small firms in January are not abnormal; the apparent January seasonal merely proxies for year-end tax-loss selling and subsequent bounceback.[7] Not all small firms will benefit from a January rebound; indiscriminately buying small firms at the turn of the year is not an optimal investment strategy. Ascertaining true causation leads to more profitable strategies.

---

[7]See Bruce I. Jacobs and Kenneth N. Levy, "Calendar Anomalies: Abnormal Returns at Calendar Turning Points," *Financial Analysts Journal* (November/ December 1988).

Return Revelation

Disentangling can reveal hidden opportunities. Exhibit 3 plots the naively measured cumulative excess returns (relative to the 3,000-stock universe) to portfolios that rank lower than average in market capitalization and price per share and higher than average in terms of analyst neglect.[8] These results derive from monthly univariate regressions. The "small-cap" line thus represents the cumulative excess returns to a portfolio of stocks naively chosen on the basis of their size, with no attempt made to control for other variables.

Exhibit 3: Naive Returns Can Hide Opportunities: Three Size-Related Variables

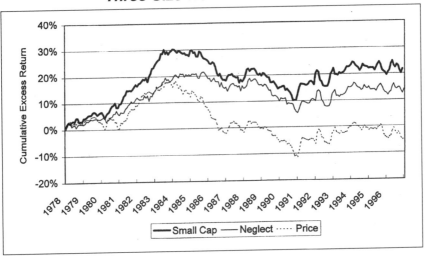

All three return series move together. The similarity between the small-cap and neglect series is particularly striking. This is confirmed by the correlation coefficients in the first column of Exhibit 4. Furthermore, all series show a great deal of volatility within a broader up, down, up pattern.

Exhibit 5 shows the pure cumulative excess returns to each size-related attribute over the period. These disentangled returns adjust for correlations not only between the three size variables, but also between each size variable and industry affiliations and each variable and growth and value characteristics. Two findings are immediately apparent from

---

[8]Again, portfolios with values of these parameters that are, on average, one standard deviation away from the universe mean.

Exhibit 5.

First, pure returns to the size variables do not appear to be near-ly as closely correlated as the naive returns displayed in Exhibit 3. In fact, over the second half of the period, the three return series diverge substantially. This is confirmed by the lower correlation coefficients in the second column of Exhibit 4.

Exhibit 4: Correlations of Monthly Returns To Size-Related Variables*

Variable	Naive	Pure
Small Cap/Low Price	0.82	−0.12
Small Cap/Neglect	0.87	−0.22
Neglect/Low Price	0.66	−0.11

*A coefficient of 0.14 is significant at the 5% level.

Exhibit 5: Pure Returns Can Reveal Opportunities: Three Size-Related Variables

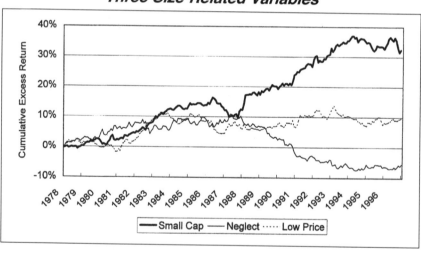

In particular, pure returns to small capitalization accumulate quite a gain over the period; they are up 30%, versus a gain of only 20% for the naive returns to small cap. Purifying returns reveals a profit opportunity not apparent in the naive returns. Furthermore, pure returns to analyst neglect amount to a substantial loss over the period. Because disentangling controls for proxy effects, and thereby avoids redundancies, these pure return effects are additive. A portfolio could have achieved truly superior returns by selecting small-cap stocks with a higher-than-average analyst following (i.e., a negative exposure to analyst neglect).

Second, the pure returns appear to be much less volatile than the naive returns. The naive returns in Exhibit 3 display much month-to-month volatility within their more general trends. By contrast, the pure series in Exhibit 5 are much smoother and more consistent. This is confirmed by the standard deviations given in Exhibit 6.

Exhibit 6: Pure Returns Are Less Volatile, More Predictable: Standard Deviations of Monthly Returns

Variable	Naive	Pure
Small Cap	0.87	0.60
Neglect	0.87	0.67
Low Price	1.03	0.58

*All differences between naive and pure return standard deviations are significant at the 1% level.

The pure returns in Exhibit 5 are smoother and more consistent than the naive return responses in Exhibit 3 because the pure returns capture more "signal" and less noise. And because they are smoother and more consistent than naive returns, pure returns are also more predictable.

Predictability

Disentangling improves return predictability by providing a clearer picture of the relationship between stock price behavior, company fundamentals, and macroeconomic conditions. For example, investors often prefer value stocks in bearish market environments, because growth stocks are priced more on the basis of high expectations, which get dashed in more pessimistic eras. But the success of such a strategy will depend on the measures one has chosen to define value.

Exhibit 7 displays the results of regressing both naive and pure returns to various value-related variables on market (S&P 500) returns over the 1978-1996 period. The results indicate that DDM value is a poor indicator of a stock's ability to withstand a tide of receding market prices. The regression coefficient in the first column indicates that a portfolio with a one-standard-deviation exposure to DDM value will tend to outperform by 0.06% when the market rises by 1.00% and to underperform by a similar margin when the market falls by 1.00%. The coefficient for pure returns to DDM is similar. Whether their returns are measured in pure or naive form, stocks with high DDM values tend to behave pro-cyclically.

Exhibit 7: Market Sensitivities of Monthly Returns To Value-Related Variables

Variable	Naive	(t-stat.)	Pure	(t-stat.)
DDM	0.06	(5.4)	0.04	(5.6)
B/P	−0.10	(−6.2)	−0.01	(−0.8)
Yield	−0.08	(−7.4)	−0.03	(−3.5)

High book-to-price ratio appears to be a better indicator of a defensive stock. It has a regression coefficient of −0.10 in naive form. In pure form, however, B/P is virtually uncorrelated with market movements; pure B/P signals neither an aggressive nor a defensive stock. B/P as naively measured apparently picks up the effects of truly defensive variables — such as high yield.

The value investor in search of a defensive posture in uncertain market climates should consider moving toward high yield. The regression coefficients for both naive and pure returns to high yield indicate significant negative market sensitivities. Stocks with high yields may be expected to lag in up markets but to hold up relatively well during general market declines.

These results make broad intuitive sense. DDM is forward-looking, relying on estimates of future earnings. In bull markets, investors take a long-term outlook, so DDM explains security pricing behavior. In bear markets, however, investors become myopic; they prefer today's tangible income to tomorrow's promise, and so current yield is rewarded.[9]

Pure returns respond in intuitively satisfying ways to macroeconomic events. Exhibit 8 illustrates, as an example, the estimated effects of changes in various macroeconomic variables on the pure returns to small size (as measured by market capitalization).

Consistent with the capital constraints on small firms and their relatively greater sensitivity to the economy, pure returns to small size may be expected to be negative in the first four months following an unexpected increase in the BAA corporate rate and positive in the first

---

[9]See also Bruce I. Jacobs and Kenneth N. Levy, "On the Value of 'Value'," *Financial Analysts Journal* (July/August 1988).

Exhibit 8: Forecast Response of Small Size To Macroeconomic Shocks

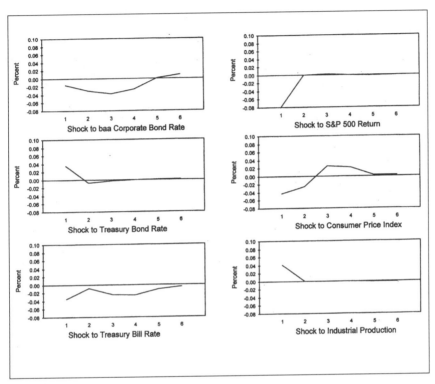

month following an unexpected increase in industrial production.[10] Investors can exploit such predictable behavior by moving into and out of the small-cap market segment as economic conditions evolve.[11]

These examples serve to illustrate that the use of numerous, finely defined fundamental variables can provide a rich representation of the complexity of security pricing. The model can be even more finely tuned, however, by including variables that capture such subtleties as the effects of investor psychology, possible nonlinearities in variable-return relationships, and security transaction costs.

---

[10]See Bruce I. Jacobs and Kenneth N. Levy, "Forecasting the Size Effect," *Financial Analysts Journal* (May/June 1989).

[11]See, for example, Bruce I. Jacobs and Kenneth N. Levy, "High-Definition Style Rotation," *Journal of Investing* (Fall 1996), pp. 14-23.

Additional Complexities

In considering possible variables for inclusion in a model of stock price behavior, it is important to recognize that pure stock returns are driven by a combination of economic fundamentals and investor psychology. That is, economic fundamentals such as interest rates, industrial production, and inflation can explain much, but by no means all, of the systematic variation in returns. Psychology — including investors' tendency to overreact, their desire to seek safety in numbers, and their selective memories — also plays a role in security pricing.

What's more, the effects of different variables, fundamental and otherwise, can differ across different types of stocks. The value sector, for example, includes more financial stocks than the growth sector. Value stocks in general may thus be expected to be more sensitive than growth stocks to changes in interest rate default spreads.

Psychologically based variables such as short-term overreaction and price correction also seem to have a stronger effect on value than on growth stocks. Earnings surprises and earnings estimate revisions, by contrast, appear to be more important for growth than for value stocks. Thus, Intel shares can take a nose dive when earnings come in a penny under expectations, whereas Ford shares remain unmoved even by fairly substantial departures of actual earnings from expectations.

The relationship between stock returns and relevant variables may not be linear. The effects of positive earnings surprises, for instance, tend to be arbitraged away quickly; thus positive earnings surprises may offer less opportunity for superior returns. The effects of negative earnings surprises, however, appear to be more long-lasting. Perhaps this is because sales of stock are limited to those investors who already own the stock (and to a relatively small number of short-sellers).[12]

Risk-variable relationships may also differ across different types of stock. In particular, small-cap stocks generally have more idiosyncratic risk than large-cap stocks. Diversification is thus more important for small-stock than for large-stock portfolios.

Return-variable relationships can also change over time. Recall the difference between DDM and yield value measures: High-DDM stocks tend to have high returns in bull markets and low returns in bear markets; high-yield stocks experience the reverse. For consistency of performance, return modeling must consider the effects of market dynamics — the changing nature of the overall market.

---

[12]See Bruce I. Jacobs and Kenneth N. Levy, "Long/Short Equity Investing," *Journal of Portfolio Management* (Fall 1993).

Finally, a complex model containing multiple variables is likely to turn up a number of promising return-variable relationships. But are these perceived profit opportunities translatable into real economic opportunities? Are some too ephemeral? Too small to survive frictions such as trading costs? Estimates of expected returns must be combined with estimates of the costs of trading to arrive at realistic returns net of trading costs.

ENGINEERING PORTFOLIOS

Security selection is just the first half of the investment management story. Insights gained in the selection process can be wasted if they are not implemented correctly. While judicious stock selection can provide excess return, portfolio construction must be conducted so as to control portfolio risk. This means that the portfolio construction (including trading) process must be as rigorous as the selection process itself.

The goal is to maximize portfolio return while controlling portfolio risk relative to the underlying benchmark. The portfolio's systematic risk should be close to that of the benchmark. The portfolio's residual risk should be no more than is justified by its expected excess return.

A broad-based approach to security valuation, one that also has the complexity to plumb the depths of security pricing behavior, provides the investment manager with the flexibility to tailor portfolios to a wide variety of client needs and the tools to fine-tune the portfolios' risks and enhance their returns relative to underlying benchmarks.[13] Portfolios can in fact be "engineered" to multiple specifications, whether those are set by the client or by underlying performance benchmarks.

Consider, for example, a pension officer who has no strong opinion about growth versus value, say, but believes that the equity market will continue to offer its average historical premium over alternative cash and bond investments. This plan may choose to hold the market in the form of a broad-based core portfolio that can deliver the all-important equity market premium (at the market's risk level). Insightful security valuation can add to that the potential for some incremental return consistent with the additional risk incurred.[14]

---

[13]See, for example, Bruce I. Jacobs and Kenneth N. Levy, "Engineering Portfolios: A Unified Approach," *Journal of Investing* (Winter 1995).

[14]For a discussion of the appropriate level of risk for an investor of a given risk aversion level with a manager of given skill, see Bruce I. Jacobs and Kenneth N. Levy, "Residual Risk: How Much is Too Much?" *Journal of Portfolio Management* (Spring 1996).

Or consider a pension officer who has a strong belief that value stocks will outperform. The investment manager can engineer a value portfolio that offers a given level of incremental return, based on the insights gleaned by the selection model, consistent with the plan's chosen level of incremental risk relative to a selected value index. In fact, with engineered portfolios, a pension plan has the ability to fine-tune overall portfolio exposures. For example, the plan can overweight growth stocks while retaining exposure to the overall market by placing some portion of the portfolio in core equity and the remainder in a growth portfolio, or by placing some percentage in a value portfolio and a larger percentage in a growth portfolio. Exposures to the market and to its various subsets can be precisely controlled.

This level of control helps to ensure portfolio integrity. Engineered style portfolios are nonoverlapping; value portfolios contain no growth stocks, nor growth portfolios any value stocks. Furthermore, the style benchmarks are, in the aggregate, inclusive of all stocks in the selection universe. The underlying benchmarks for value and growth portfolios, say, or for large- and small-cap portfolios, will aggregate to the equity core. The plan can be assured of complete coverage of the equity universe.

Expanding Opportunities

Model insights are perhaps best exploited by portfolios that are not constrained to deliver a benchmark-like performance — by portfolios that are free to pursue the expected rewards from the model's insights, constrained only by the client's risk preferences.

For example, portfolios tied to a particular style benchmark will fall behind the overall market when that particular style is out of favor. The historical evidence suggests that any given style will tend to outperform the overall market in some periods and to underperform it in others. A style-rotation strategy seeks to deliver returns in excess of the market's by forecasting style subset performance and shifting investment weights aggressively among various style subsets as market and economic conditions evolve.

Style rotation takes advantage of the entire selection universe. A style-rotation portfolio can be engineered to offer a level of incremental return commensurate with a pension plan's level of risk aversion. Rotation among passive style indexes may be able to offer incremental returns above the overall market return, at moderate levels of incremental risk. But a plan that chooses to take advantage of the complex model's ability to disentangle style attributes and fine-tune style may expect even higher returns for not much more risk.

Allowing short sales, whether in conjunction with a core portfolio, a style portfolio, or style rotation, can further enhance return opportunities. While traditional management focuses on the selection of "winning" securities, the breadth of a complex quantitative approach allows the client to profit from "losers" as well as "winners." With an engineered portfolio that allows shorting of losers, the manager can pursue potential mispricings without constraint, going long underpriced stocks and selling short overpriced stocks.

In markets in which short selling is not widespread, there are reasons to believe that shorting stocks can offer more opportunity than buying stocks. This is because restrictions on short selling do not permit investor pessimism to be as fully represented in prices as investor optimism. In such a market, the potential candidates for short sale may be less efficiently priced, hence offer greater return potential, than the potential candidates for purchase.[15]

Shorting can enhance performance by eliminating constraints on the implementation of investment insights. Consider, for example, that a security with a median market capitalization has a weighting of approximately 0.01% of the market's capitalization. Without shorting, a manager can underweight such a security by, at most, 0.01% relative to the market; this is achieved by not holding the security at all.

Those who do not consider this unduly restrictive should consider that placing a like constraint on the maximum portfolio overweight would be equivalent to saying the manager could hold, at most, a 0.02% position in the stock, no matter how appetizing its expected return. Shorting allows the manager free rein in translating the insights gained from the stock selection process into portfolio performance.

Long-Short Portfolios

If security returns are symmetrically distributed about the underlying market return, there will be fully as many unattractive securities for short sale as there are attractive securities for purchase. The manager can construct a portfolio that balances equal dollar amounts and equal systematic risks long and short. Such a long-short balance neutralizes the risk (and return) of the underlying market. The portfolio's return — which can be measured as the spread between the long and short returns

---

[15]See, for example, Bruce I. Jacobs and Kenneth N. Levy, "20 Myths About Long-Short," *Financial Analysts Journal* (September/October 1996).

— is solely reflective of the manager's skill at stock selection.[16]

Not only does such a long-short portfolio neutralize underlying market risk, it offers improved control of residual risk relative to a long-only portfolio. For example, the long-only portfolio can control risk relative to the underlying benchmark only by converging toward the weights of the benchmark's stocks; these weights constrain portfolio composition. Balancing securities' sensitivities long and short, however, eliminates risk relative to the underlying benchmark; benchmark weights are thus not constraining in long-short. Furthermore, the long-short portfolio can use offsetting long and short positions to fine-tune the portfolio's residual risk.

In addition to enhanced return and improved risk control, an engineered long-short approach also offers clients added flexibility in asset allocation. A simple long-short portfolio, for example, offers a return from security selection on top of a cash return (that is, the interest received on the proceeds from the short sales). However, the long-short portfolio can also be combined with a position in derivatives such as stock index futures. Such an "equitized" portfolio will offer the long-short portfolio's security selection return on top of the equity market return provided by the futures position; choice of other available derivatives can provide the return from security selection in combination with exposure to other asset classes. The transportability of the long-short portfolio's return offers pension plans the ability to take advantage of a manager's security selection skills while determining independently the plan's asset allocation mix.

A Customized Optimizer

To maximize implementation of the selection model's insights, the portfolio construction process should consider exactly the same dimensions found relevant by the stock selection model. Failure to do so can lead to mismatches between model insights and portfolio exposures.

Consider a commercially available portfolio optimizer that recognizes only a subset of the variables in the valuation model. Risk reduction using such an optimizer will reduce the portfolio's exposures only along the dimensions the optimizer recognizes. As a result, the portfolio is like-

---

[16]See Bruce I. Jacobs and Kenneth N. Levy, "The Long and Short on Long-Short," *Journal of Investing* (Spring 1997), pp. 73-86. See also Bruce I. Jacobs, Kenneth N. Levy, and David Starer, "On the Optimality of Long-Short Strategies," *Financial Analysts Journal* (March/April 1998), for an analysis of long-short balance.

ly to wind up more exposed to those variables recognized by the model — but not the optimizer — and less exposed to those variables common to both the model and the optimizer.

Imagine a manager who seeks low-P/E stocks that analysts are recommending for purchase, but who uses a commercial optimizer that incorporates a P/E factor but not analyst recommendations. The investor is likely to wind up with a portfolio that has a less than optimal level of exposure to low P/E and a greater than optimal level of exposure to analyst purchase recommendations. Optimization using all relevant variables ensures a portfolio whose risk and return opportunities are balanced in accordance with the selection model's insights. Furthermore, the use of more numerous variables allows portfolio risk to be more finely tuned.

Insofar as the investment process, both stock selection and portfolio construction, is model-driven, it is more adaptable to electronic trading venues. This should benefit a pension plan in several ways. First, electronic trading is generally less costly, with lower commissions, market impact, and opportunity costs. Second, it allows real-time monitoring, which can further reduce trading costs. Third, an automated trading system can take account of more factors, including the urgency of a particular trade and market conditions, than individual traders can be expected to bear in mind.

The performance attribution process should also be congruent with the dimensions of the selection model (and portfolio optimizer). Insofar as performance attribution identifies sources of return, a process that considers all the sources identified by the selection model will be more insightful than a commercial performance attribution system applied in a "one size fits all" manner. The manager who has sought exposure to low P/E and positive analyst recommendations, for example, will want to know how each of these factors has paid off and will be less interested in the returns to factors that are not a part of the stock selection process.

A performance evaluation process tailored to the selection model also functions as a monitor of the model's reliability. Has portfolio performance supported the model's insights? Equally important, does the model's reliability hold up over time? A model that performs well in today's economic and market environments may not necessarily perform well in the future. A feedback loop between the evaluation and the research/modeling processes can help ensure that the model retains robustness over time.

PROFITING FROM COMPLEXITY

It has been said that: "For every complex problem, there's a simple solution, and it's almost always wrong."[17]

A complex approach to stock selection, portfolio construction, and performance evaluation is needed to capture the complexities of the stock market. Such an approach combines the breadth of coverage and the depth of analysis needed to maximize investment opportunity and potential reward.

Grinold and Kahn present a formula that identifies the relationships between the depth and breadth of investment insights and investment performance:

$$IR = IC \ x \ \sqrt{BR}$$

IR is the manager's information ratio, a measure of the success of the investment process. IR equals annualized excess return over annualized residual risk (e.g., 2% excess return with 4% tracking error provides 0.5 IR). IC, the information coefficient, or correlation between predicted and actual results, measures the goodness of the manager's insights, or the manager's skill. BR is the breadth of the strategy, measurable as the number of independent insights upon which investment decisions are made.[18]

One can increase IR by increasing IC or BR. Increasing IC means developing some means of improving predictive accuracy. Increasing BR means discovering more "investable" insights. A casino analogy may be apt (if anathema to prudent investors).

A gambler can seek to increase IC by card-counting in blackjack or by building a computer model to predict probable roulette outcomes. Similarly, some investors seek to outperform by concentrating their research efforts on a few stocks: By learning all there is to know about Microsoft, for example, one may be able to outperform all the other investors who follow this stock. But a strategy that makes a few concentrated stock bets is likely to produce consistent performance only if it is based on a very high level of skill, or if it benefits from extraordinary luck.

Alternatively, an investor can place a larger number of smaller stock bets and settle for more modest returns from a greater number of

---

[17]Attributed to H.L. Mencken.

[18]Richard C. Grinold and Ronald N. Kahn, *Active Portfolio Management* (Chicago, IL: Probus, 1995).

investment decisions. That is, rather than behaving like a gambler in a casino, the investor can behave like the casino. A casino has only a slight edge on any spin of the roulette wheel or roll of the dice, but many spins of many roulette wheels can result in a very consistent profit for the house. Over time, the odds will strongly favor the casino over the gambler.

A complex approach to the equity market, one that has both breadth of inquiry and depth of focus, can enhance both the number and the goodness of investment insights and the implementation of those insights. It thus helps to ensure that the active equity investor enjoys excess returns, and not excessive risks.

Thomas K. Philips is chief investment officer of Paradigm Asset Management, a domestic equity manager with over $1.7 billion under management. Philips is responsible for all aspects of the investment process, including the development of new products and the enhancement of existing ones.

Prior to joining Paradigm Investment Management, Philips was managing director at Symphony Asset Management and its predecessor, RogersCasey Alternative Investments, with shared responsibilities at Rogers, Casey and Associates. He conducted research on various aspects of public and private markets, and selected venture capital and buyout funds for investment by clients of RogersCasey.

Previously, Philips spent eight years at IBM Corp. For his first five years he conducted research on problems in operations, computer science, and applied mathematics at the IBM Thomas J. Watson Research Center. His last three years at IBM were spent at the retirement fund in Stanford, Conn., in the investment research and active equity management groups.

Philips received his bachelor of science degree in electrical engineering from Benares Hindu University in Varanasi, India, and his master of science degree and Ph.D. in electrical and computer engineering from the University of Massachusetts at Amherst, where he was elected a fellow of the graduate school. He has published numerous journal papers and three book chapters on topics in finance, engineering, and mathematics.

Chapter 4

The Pros and Cons of Indexing Pension Assets

Thomas K. Philips, Ph.D.
Chief Investment Officer
Paradigm Asset Management

Thirty years ago, a plan sponsor who talked of indexing his or her portfolio would have encountered bewilderment. The term "index fund" had not as yet been coined, and only a few academics would have had any understanding of what the plan sponsor was attempting to do and his reasons for doing so. Peter Bernstein[1] suggests that Wells Fargo Bank first used the term in its modern sense when it started running an S&P 500 index fund for the Samsonite Corporation's pension fund.

Keith Schwayder, a member of the family that owned the luggage manufacturer, attended the University of Chicago and learned about indexing in a course on finance. When he returned to work at Samsonite, he urged the pension fund to exploit ideas on the frontiers of finance, and promptly hired Wells Fargo to run a $6 million S&P 500 index fund.

From these humble beginnings, the world of index funds has grown relentlessly. By the middle of 1996, institutional investors had committed over $730 billion to index funds of various kinds. The S&P 500 index was the single most widely used index with over $450 billion of capital committed to it. These numbers are significant, and strongly suggest that the phenomenon of investing in index funds is not a passing fad or fancy.

In this chapter, we explore the pros and cons of indexing and the interplay between indexing and active management. We start by precisely defining indexing and then explore the rich history of ideas that underlies it. In particular, we examine the connection between the notions of market efficiency and indexing. Next, we explore the role of indexes in a wide range of markets: domestic equities and fixed income, international and emerging markets, commodities and alternative invest-

---

1. Peter Bernstein, *Capital Ideas* (New York: The Free Press, 1992).

ments. Following this, we explore the pros and cons of indexing and the corresponding implications for active management in each of these areas. Finally, we summarize our thoughts and draw conclusions.

WHAT IS INDEXING AND WHY IS IT IMPORTANT?

A short list of definitions makes this topic far easier to discuss. First, we define a market to be a set of freely traded securities that may be bought or sold at any time. The market portfolio is a portfolio of securities in which each security is held in proportion to its value outstanding or its market capitalization. An example will clarify this.

Suppose the entire market consists of two stocks: call them IBM and GE. IBM has 100 shares outstanding and these shares are traded at $100 apiece. GE has 200 shares outstanding and these shares are traded at $75 apiece. IBM's market capitalization or the value of its shares outstanding is $100 × 100 = $10,000, and GE's market capitalization is $75 × 200 = $15,000. The market portfolio is 10,000/(10,000 + 15,000) = 40% IBM and 15,000/(10,000 + 15,000) = 60% GE. Notice that as the prices of IBM and GE fluctuate, their relative weight in the market portfolio changes correspondingly and, assuming no changes in the composition of the index, there is never any need to rebalance the portfolio after it is first established.

An index fund holds a predetermined subset of the securities that comprise the market in proportion to their market capitalization. Some indexes, such as the S&P 500 or the Russell 3000, attempt to mimic the market portfolio by holding a large number of representative securities. Others, such as the S&P 400 Growth Index and the Russell 1000 Value Index hold a set of securities that meet some criteria for size and stock fundamentals (for example, the ratio of book value to stock price).

Indexing is an important concept because investors in aggregate cannot outperform the market portfolio. The reason for this is simple: the sum of all investors' portfolios must equal the market portfolio. Therefore the weighted sum of all investors' returns must equal the return of the market portfolio. Relative to the market portfolio, investing is a zero-sum game: Some investors outperform the market if and only if other investors underperform the market.

A balloon provides a particularly elegant exposition of this point. Suppose that the wealth contained in all the securities that comprise a market is laid out on the surface of a balloon. Each individual investor will lay claim to a patch that represents his or her holdings. Clearly, the sum of all investors' holdings must equal the entire market.

Now let the market rise or fall by inflating or deflating the balloon. If the balloon has no patches of unusual thickness, the entire surface will grow or shrink at the same rate. It follows that all investors' portfolios must grow at roughly the same rate as the market. The market portfolio corresponds to the surface of the balloon, and this example shows that most investors will find it difficult to outperform the market.

A Brief Overview of Efficient Market Theory

The balloon model of capital markets described in the last section can be developed into a comprehensive mathematical theory of market efficiency, which asserts that most securities are fairly priced most of the time, and that their price reflects the risk they bear. A logical consequence of this theory is that investors can outperform the market only by taking on more risk. This philosophy of investing requires investors to make an asset allocation decision among different classes of securities, and to then implement their allocation using index funds in each asset class.

In recent years, however, some cracks have begun to appear in the theory of efficient markets.[2] Researchers have identified a number of anomalies that seem to allow excess returns without assuming excess risks. The small-cap effect, the January effect and the book to price effect are three concrete examples of anomalies that have been identified in the capital markets. The persistence of these anomalies, however, varies. As they become more widely known and understood, investors arbitrage them away.

An investor who can consistently identify market anomalies will often prefer active management to indexing. Conversely, an investor who cannot consistently identify market anomalies will always prefer indexing to active management. Some investors who can identify market anomalies will still prefer to index their money because transaction costs and fees can erode any informational advantage they have. As a result, the pros and cons of indexing will depend on the segment of the market under review.

A SURVEY OF INDEXING IN VARIOUS DOMESTIC MARKETS

Equities

The domestic equity market has a total capitalization of close to $8 tril-

---

[2]George M. Frankfurter, "The Rise and Fall of the CAPM Empire: A Review on Emerging Capital Markets," *Financial Markets, Institutions and Instruments* 4 (1995): 104-127.

lion (as of March 31, 1997) and is tracked by a wide range of indices. The most famous of these is the Standard & Poors 500 Stock Index, a collection of 500 stocks that accounts for roughly two-thirds of the total capitalization of the domestic equity market and is chosen by a committee to mirror the composition of the market.

Other indices track segments of the market: the small-cap sector, the mid-cap sector, and the large-cap sector, the growth-and-value sectors, and various industry sectors. Institutional investors can index their money in most sectors for an annual fee of about five basis points. In addition, futures on a number of equity indices are traded on futures exchanges, allowing investors to implement an index with a single transaction.

Sector and style indices allow investors to implement their market views at low cost, and provide benchmarks for active implementations of these views. One investor might wish to have a strong value tilt to his portfolio based on the long run return to value stocks, while another might wish to implement a size tilt based on her view that small capitalization stocks are undervalued relative to their large capitalization counterparts. A third investor may hold no view on the relative valuation of the various market sectors but finds style indices invaluable in monitoring the performance of the style specific active managers retained by him.

Fixed Income

The domestic fixed-income market is richer, deeper, and even more liquid than the domestic equity market and once again a wide range of indexes exist. The two most widely used indexes are the Lehman Aggregate Index and the Salomon Broad Investment Grade Index. Both attempt to mirror the composition of the entire fixed income market, with large holdings in corporate bonds and mortgages.

Indexes exist to track market segments by maturity, quality and type of issuer. For example, the Lehman Corporate Bond Index contains a wide range of bonds issued by corporations. These bonds must have a maturity greater than one year and a credit rating greater than A. The mortgage sector has a particularly rich set of indices that track both whole loans and collateralized mortgage obligations. Futures trade mainly on government bonds, Eurodollars, and certain interest rate contracts. As a result, it is somewhat harder to implement an index fund using futures than in the equity markets.

Commodities

Commodity indexes differ from all other indices in that they are based on derivatives, typically futures contracts, instead of the underlying physical assets. Defining a commodity index in this manner has two great advantages:

- The investor is not required to hold any physical commodities. (Storing pork bellies can be difficult, if not impossible!)
- The return earned by the future is typically higher than the return earned by the underlying physical commodity, as futures often trade at a discount to the underlying spot commodity. This happens because it is difficult, if not impossible, to arbitrage mispricings in commodity markets.

The Goldman Sachs Commodity Index is the most widely quoted index of commodities, and is composed of a wide range of commodities that are weighted in proportion to their production. As the index definition includes buying new commodity contracts every month or two, it takes much more effort to duplicate a commodity index than an equity or fixed income index. The management fees associated with commodity indices are therefore are an order of magnitude higher than those associated with equity and fixed-income indices.

Alternative Investments (Private Equity)

This area is most unusual in that no well-defined index exists. The transparency that public market investors take for granted has not yet permeated the world of private equity. Fund managers typically disclose information on their funds to investors only when they are raising money for a new fund. As private equity funds are not publicly traded, there is no central clearing house or exchange that can collate information on the private equity industry. Venture Economics, a Boston-based company has tried to bridge this gap by obtaining information on cash flows from limited partners and then collating this information to construct indexes[3].

In recent years, some general partner groups have become more liberal with data, and provide it to Venture Economics directly. Indexes are constructed by vintage year — all funds that raised capital in a given year are said to be of that vintage, or to belong to the same cohort. The

---

[3]*Investment Benchmarks Report: Buyouts, Mezzanine and Special Situations Partnerships* and *Investment Benchmarks Report: Venture Capital* (Boston: Venture Economics, 1997).

performance of these funds is then tracked throughout their lives by Venture Economics, and the "index" is defined to be the set of all funds for which data is available. Observe that this index is not observable: no one knows ahead of time which funds will supply information to Venture Economics. Furthermore, the set of funds that discloses results to Venture Economics can and does change over time, leading to corresponding changes in the composition of the index. In spite of these limitations, we believe that the Venture Economics indexes are a good starting point and should be used to benchmark the performance of a private equity program.

THE PROS AND CONS OF INDEXING

Earlier in this chapter we modeled the capital markets by a balloon, and used this model to show that investors in aggregate could not outperform the market. We now extend this argument further to show that active managers in aggregate must underperform the market. The set of all investors can be decomposed into two groups — indexers and active managers. Indexers earn market returns, so that after transaction costs, active investors in aggregate must underperform the market.

The case for active management therefore rests on the answer to four questions:

- Does the market contain inefficiencies that can be identified by superior investors?
- Is the cost of exploiting these inefficiencies low enough to warrant trying?
- Can investors identify active managers who can outperform the market?
- Is the index easily implemented at low cost?

If the answer to all four questions is yes, active management is preferable to indexing. If not, indexing is preferable to active management. The first question must almost always be answered in the affirmative for the following reason. Suppose there are no inefficiencies. Then active management would make no sense, and investors, being rational, would expend no energy on active management. The fact that they do, and that some consistently succeed (Warren Buffet is the quintessential example), is evidence for the presence of some inefficiency.

The answer to the second and third question depends on the market under consideration. However, we can reformulate the third question in a way that makes it more amenable to analysis. To do so, we first take a step back and ask if we can identify managers who have in the past out-performed the market more by skill than by luck. Our answer is yes, and the key to identifying managers who have done well in the past is to mea-sure their information ratio, or the ratio of their excess return relative to an appropriate index to their tracking error relative to the same index. The tracking error is defined to be the standard deviation of the excess return.

If we make the simple assumption that the manager's excess returns are normally distributed, a manager with an information ratio of zero outperforms the benchmark purely by luck; a manager with an infor-mation ratio of 0.25 has roughly a 2/3 chance of outperforming his bench-mark over a period of three to five years; a manager with an information ratio of 0.5 has roughly a 5/6 chance of outperforming his benchmark over the same period; and a manager with an information ratio of 1 is almost certain to outperform his benchmark. It is our experience that informa-tion ratios substantially greater than 1 are not the result of skill, but of a large bet (typically on a few stocks or industry sectors) that the manag-er took. Such a bet is likely to reverse itself sharply at some point. Exhibit 1 shows the exact probabilities of beating a benchmark over peri-ods of one, three, and five years as a function of the information ratio.

Exhibit 1: Probability of Outperforming the Benchmark Versus Information Ratio and Time Horizon

Information Ratio	Probability that the Manager Outperforms the Benchmark		
	1 Year	3 Years	5 Years
0.00	0.50	0.50	0.50
0.25	0.60	0.67	0.71
0.50	0.69	0.81	0.87
1.00	0.84	0.96	0.99

By computing a given manager's information ratio, one can determine the likelihood that his results were the result of skill instead of luck. We can now rephrase our third question as "Are past information ratios predictive of future information ratios?" If the answer is yes, active management is the preferred investment strategy; if no, indexing is the strategy of choice. We examine each market separately, and provide answers to each of these four questions whenever possible.

Equities

The domestic equity market is generally considered to be the world's most efficient equity market. Active managers have found it very difficult to outperform broad market benchmarks such as the S&P 500. In fact, it was the examination of active manager performance relative to the domestic equity market that first lent credence to academic claims of market efficiency.[4]

Recently, however, evidence for the persistence of performance has been found. In his 1996 presidential address to the American Finance Association, Professor Martin Gruber showed that mutual fund performance showed remarkable persistence after controlling for the presence of cash, bonds, and equity-style bets in the portfolio.[5] This suggests that it makes sense to invest with style-specific active managers who have consistently demonstrated the ability to outperform their benchmark.

A broad market benchmark can be addressed in one of two ways: passively through an index fund or using a combination of style-specific active managers to construct a portfolio that matches the index's risk characteristics while adding value. Indexing is extremely cheap — management fees are on the order of five basis points per annum, and can be done either in the cash or futures market.

Enhanced Indexing Enhanced indexing, or risk-controlled active management, is particularly attractive in the domestic equity market. Enhanced index portfolios take small bets relative to their benchmark, never overweighting or underweighting any given security or sector by more than a few percent. An optimizer is used to construct an efficient frontier and the portfolio is chosen to lie on this frontier. By a judicious choice of constraints and operating point, the portfolio can be made to track the benchmark closely while adding value through sector and security selection.

Fixed Income

Because of its depth and liquidity, the fixed-income market is extremely efficient, suggesting that indexing is preferable to active management. Two factors mitigate against this conclusion. First, there is strong evidence of persistence in the returns of fixed-income managers, even

---

[4]Eugene Fama, "Efficient Capital Markets II," *Journal of Finance* (December 1991): 1575-1617.

[5]Martin Gruber, "Another Puzzle: The Growth in Actively Managed Mutual Funds" *Journal of Finance* (July 1996): 783-810.

though managers on average underperform their benchmark.[6] Second, managers can add value by overweighting sectors (such as the mortgage and corporate sectors) which trade at a positive yield spread to treasuries. As an added bonus, the inefficiency in these sectors is larger than that in the Treasury sector.

If one wishes to replicate the sector exposures of a benchmark exactly, an index fund is probably the better alternative. If, on the other hand, one is willing to take on some additional risk, active management looks attractive. Indexes are easy to implement but, because a typical bond index contains many thousands of securities, small accounts (say those under $100 million) are perhaps best placed in a commingled vehicle.

Commodities

Commodity indexes are sufficiently new that there are very few active managers who manage commodity futures. Most active managers (or commodity trading advisers as they are referred to) run hedge fund like products with little or no risk control and substantial amounts of leverage. Their fees are high — on the order of a 1% base fee with a 20% participation in the profits. For these reasons, we would be extremely cautious about hiring active managers for commodities. A few managers have started to develop risk controlled active management processes, and we would watch carefully to see what results they obtain before making any commitments to active management.

As the commodity index is defined using futures, it is not static. The futures must be rolled every month and the index is constantly evolving. In effect, the index itself is an active portfolio, and the cost of indexing is substantially higher than the cost of indexing equities or fixed income.

Alternative Investments (Private Equity)

As noted earlier, this area is most unusual in that no well-defined index exists. It is therefore not possible to invest in an index fund. One possible alternative is to simply commit some capital to all funds that are raising money. Because of a fundamental difference between public and private markets, this investment strategy is almost guaranteed to do poorly.

In a freely traded capital market, prices can adapt upward or downward to reflect a firm's future prospects. If the prospects are poor and the management is weak, the price drops so that expected future returns adequately compensate the buyer for risk. With private equity,

---

[6]Ronald N. Kahn and Andrew Rudd, "Does Historical Performance Predict Future Performance?" *Financial Analysts Journal* (Nov.-Dec. 1995): 43-52.

however, all venture capitalists offer roughly the same terms (2% per annum management fee and 20% participation in all profits), so the quality of the management team is not reflected in the price of the investment.

Arguably, the easiest way to do poorly in an alternative investment program is to invest in all available funds in an index-like fashion. The volume of work associated with such a strategy is overwhelming, and it is very tempting to reduce one's workload by signing documents without scrutinizing them or negotiating terms and conditions. This is a recipe for disaster. To further complicate matters, the number of distributions received is directly proportional to the number of fund investments. We strongly recommend the use of active management in this area.[7]

SUMMARY AND CONCLUSIONS

In this chapter we have explored the pros and cons of indexing in the major domestic asset classes. In some asset classes, such as equities and fixed income, broad markets are best indexed, while specialized sector specific mandates can be addressed both by indexers and active managers. We strongly suggest the use of enhanced indexing or risk-controlled active management because it allows active managers to add value without taking on undue risks.

In commodities, risk-controlled active management has a short history, and we would urge investors to index their money. In private equity, we feel that indexing is a fundamentally bad way to invest, and that active management is better by far.

Regardless of how one invests, it is vital to monitor the managers one hires and to ensure that their investment process remains stable over time. With active managers in particular, it is imperative that the portfolio be examined at regular intervals to detect any potential problems before they arise. With careful oversight, it is possible to deliver good performance using both index funds and active managers, and the decision to use one or the other should be made on the basis of the investor's needs and the availability of suitable products and services.

---

[7]Thomas K. Philips, "A Portfolio Approach to Alternative Investments," RogersCasey Alternative Investments Research Report (1995).

Nancy C. Nakovick joined Bear Stearns & Co. in October 1997 as a vice president in portfolio trading. Nakovick is a seasoned plan sponsor and consultant on pension investment strategies, with special expertise in the use of derivatives and portfolio trading.

Much of the research included in this chapter was performed while Nakovick was with the New York office of Société Générale as vice president of sales and co-head of research for the equity derivatives group. In this capacity, she specialized in selling and structuring derivative strategies for pension funds, insurance companies, and money managers. Nakovick also sat on Société Générale's pension committee.

Prior to Société Générale, Nakovick worked in equity derivatives research at Goldman Sachs.

Nakovick has been dealing with derivative strategies since she first worked as a corporate finance manager at NYNEX in 1987. She acquired both domestic and international pension management experience at NYNEX and subsequently at Texaco. Nakovick developed Texaco's asset-allocation and risk-management programs using options and futures. She also ran a $200 million domestic equity portfolio in-house.

Nakovick holds a bachelor of science degree in mechanical engineering from Drexel University, a master of science degree in mechanical engineering from the Massachusetts Institute of Technology, and a master's degree in business administration from the Wharton School of the University of Pennsylvania.

Chapter 5

Management Strategies in a Changing Market

Nancy C. Nakovick
Vice President, Portfolio Trading
Bear Stearns & Co.

This chapter focuses on appropriate asset-allocation and transition management strategies for public pension plans in a changing market environment. The sections on funding and increasing stock market volatility explore the nature of a changing market from both a funding and capital markets perspective.

Over the last few years, public pension plans have been increasing benefits at a rate that far exceeds the corresponding rise in inflation. In conjunction with a tendency toward overallocation to fixed income, the average public plan sponsor has felt particularly challenged to achieve his funding objectives. Going forward, with low interest rates expected to persist and with low correlations but high volatilities across markets, plan sponsors may continue to find it difficult to achieve their investment hurdle rates.

A section on suggested investment guidelines identifies the keys to healthy public plans as consistent contributions and maintaining an asset mix designed to reduce underfunding by including a heavy weighting toward equities.

Periodically, plan assets need to be rebalanced. As described in the section on allocation to passive overlay, TAA, and/or global multiasset manager, this can be done either passively or actively. TAA (tactical asset allocation) managers should perform well, since participating markets are expected to have low correlations and remain volatile.

The section on derivatives as strategic asset-allocation and hedging tools explores alternative uses of derivatives beyond their being hedging vehicles. Plan sponsors wanting to retain discretion and flexibility might consider the use of derivatives to facilitate both strategic and tactical asset allocation.

Traditional transition management strategies focuses on ways that internal and external money managers can use traditional transition-management strategies — including EFP (exchange-for-physical) or basis trading. An active or passive overlay manager who uses derivatives as implementation vehicles can also efficiently facilitate manager transitions. Alternatively, a completion fund can be used not only for this purpose but also as a risk-reduction tool.

Sections on style management and appropriate benchmarks and completion fund as a risk-reduction tool and manager transition vehicle discuss how to construct a portfolio of manager's, while avoiding unintended style bets. Finally, the Eternal Quest for Alpha describes potentially higher "alpha" strategies including market-neutral. Since market-neutral performance, by definition, is not contingent on what is happening in the overall market, it is impervious to the effects of high market volatility.

The strategies discussed in this chapter address not only the alleviation of underfunding but also ways to maintain flexibility, particularly important during periods of above-average market volatility. Flexibility will allow pension plans to achieve their risk/return objectives while responding to changing plan demographics and the periodic need to execute manager transitions.

FUNDING

There are several reasons why public fund officials are concerned about the underfunded status of employee retirement systems, according to Olivia S. Mitchell and Robert S. Smith.[1] Public employee retirement system (PERS) borrowing could affect future government revenue-raising potentials. If workers or unions perceive underfunding as a threat to their future pensions, then underfunding could prompt them to require a compensating salary increase, resulting in increased pension contributions and, more than likely, causing funding levels to deteriorate further. Consequently, unionized employers are less likely to fully fund future pension obligations. Conversely, the Mitchell-Smith empirical model indicates that wages should fall if funding improves. Because the public sector workforce is maturing along with the rest of the population, PERS funding practices take on increasing importance.

The article by Mitchell and Smith concludes that actuarial assumptions were not manipulated to reduce employers' pension contributions. This conclusion is based on the "reasonableness" of the spreads used by plans in their 1989 dataset, which covered about half of all public-sector workers. "Spread" refers to the difference between the long-term actuarial rate of return on assets and the wage growth-rate assumption. No inference is made regarding the sample's ability to achieve this return

[1]Olivia S. Mitchell and Robert K. Smith, "Pension Funding in the Public Sector" *Review of Economics and Statistics* (May 1994): 278-90.

assumption using past or projected investment performance. In 1989, the average projected benefited obligation (PBO) funding ratio was 84%.

A July 1995 *Pension Management* article indicated that unfunded public fund pension liability totaled $200 billion.[2] Roger Smith of Greenwich Associates is quoted as saying that it would take the average public fund 27 years to amortize this liability. Only 4% could amortize unfunded liabilities in less than 10 years and 18% would need 40 years or longer. The average public fund pays 50% more pension benefits than the average private-sector plan. These public funds are also increasing benefits far more rapidly than the inflation rate at a time when the markets are less likely to cooperate. The article goes on to say that, in 1994, 67% of public funds raised benefits; some even approved benefit increases retroactively.

Many plans have improved their funding ratio since 1989, with average PBO funding growing to 90% in 1992. Nearly half of the largest state pension funds still have actuarial interest rates above expected investment portfolio returns — reflecting a tendency toward an over-allocation to fixed income.

Pension funded status is more sensitive to changes in interest rates than to changes in asset returns. A drop of one percentage point in the discount rate increases liabilities by 1% × the liability duration. As of August 1997, the Lehman Brothers Long Term Bond Yield was around 6.67%. This was 21 basis points below its level of 6.88% at the beginning of 1997. With no other changes in benefit assumptions — and with pension liabilities having a duration of around 15 years — if interest rates remained at the August level through year-end 1997, liabilities could be expected to increase by approximately 3%.

Even if a modest increase in interest rates occurred before year-end, the funded status of the median public pension plan could still be challenged. This is only in part due to an asset mix with an overallocation to fixed-income responding unfavorably to rising interest rates. In light of tight labor market conditions entering 1998, there will probably be an increase in the wage growth assumption and at least the possibility of increased benefits which, in conjunction with relatively low interest rates, will negatively impact liabilities.

---

[2]Steve Bergsman, "Public Funds in the Red: How Shaky a Foundation" *Pension Management* (July 1995): 44-47.

STOCK MARKET VOLATILITY

For the period ending December 1996, three-year and five-year volatilities for the S&P 500 have been lower than volatilities associated with longer time periods. Specifically, three-year volatility was around 8.5% and 10-year at 14%. As of August 1997, three-year volatility had increased to around 10.3%. A significant increase in volatility for the year ending August 1997 contributed to the increase in three-year volatility from December 1996 to August 1997.

Term Structure of Volatility

Just as inferences, guarded though they may be, can be drawn from the forward rates embedded in an interest rate yield curve as to the future level of interest rates, inferences can also be drawn from the term structure of volatility, regarding expectations for future volatility levels embedded in the prices of at-the-money S&P 500 options of various maturities. In general, implied option volatility tends to react to recent trading patterns and is not necessarily a good forecast for the absolute level of future underlying market volatility. What is informative is how the term structure curve moves and/or changes shape over time.

From January 1996 through August 1997, the S&P 500 term structure of volatility was as shown in Exhibit 1. As of August 1997, implied volatilities were between 19% and 21% across maturities. Since the fourth quarter of 1996, the term structure has been shifting upward and has, on average, remained normal in shape, with some degree of flat-

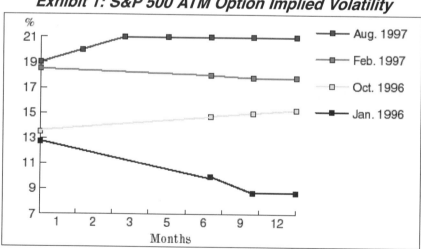

Exhibit 1: S&P 500 ATM Option Implied Volatility

tening. Rising markets and lower-than-normal volatility tend to accompany upward sloping term structures. During 1997 we saw a rising market and higher-than-normal volatility. Irrespective of the direction that the underlying market eventually takes, it is safe to say that volatility in the United States will remain high and is likely to revert to historical levels at some point in the future. In other major markets in Europe, the term structures are flatter across maturities, with volatility levels exceeding 20%.

INVESTMENT GUIDELINES

The appropriate asset allocation not only satisfies a pension plan's risk/return objectives but is determined by integrating plan demographics and calculated liabilities with expected asset returns and correlations. Based on these assumptions, this chapter offers suggestions regarding asset classes and asset ranges to help plan sponsors achieve faster — yet prudent — growth in assets to meet future obligations. These suggestions are summarized in Exhibit 2. In general, irrespective of any sort of overlay strategy as discussed below, equities should be around 50%-60% of assets. Included in this range is a 15%-20% allocation to international and emerging markets.

According to an article in the January 6, 1997, issue of *Pensions & Investments* magazine,[3] among both corporate and public pension plans, international assets have on average a 12.8% allocation, mostly in

Exhibit 2: Suggested Guidelines

Asset Class	Percentage Range (%)	Example Allocation (%)
Equities	50-60	55
Domestic	30-45	40
International	15-20	15
Bonds	20-25	20
TAA/Passive Overlay/Multi-asset	15-20	15
Real Estate/Alternative	0-20	10

[3]Margaret Price, "Foreign Investments Grow: Institutions now have 12.8% Allocation to Non-US Assets" *Pensions & Investments* vol. 25 (January 6, 1997): 3.

international equities. Between 20% and 30% of equities could be passively managed. More recently, some plan sponsors and their consultants have felt more comfortable with an even larger allocation.

In a full market cycle, studies have shown, active management can outperform passive management on a cost-effective, risk-adjusted basis.[4] Several studies have also suggested considering passive or enhanced index management for a portion of the large-cap equity allocation. This segment has optimal investible indices and highly liquid derivative instruments, often employed in index management to equitize cash and to rebalance portfolios back to index weights.

Passive Management Aspects

Within the passively managed international portion, sponsors might consider focusing on the larger, more liquid countries. These are obviously countries having the largest index weights (in EAFE, for example) and therefore the greatest potential impact on performance. For the smaller countries, the lower weighting tends to negate any outperformance benefits in terms of impacting overall portfolio return. Transaction costs in these smaller countries tend to be higher because many of the stocks are less liquid and less frequently traded. Included in this group are countries that are not considered to be emerging and therefore lack the growth potential that is normally associated with stellar investment returns.

The Active Segment

Aggregating an insufficiently diverse group of managers can often lead to unintended style bets. A completion fund, as a risk-control vehicle, allows sponsors greater flexibility to hire managers based more on skill than on style. Having recently received a favorable ruling by the Internal Revenue Service, plan sponsors can also evaluate the use of market-neutral strategies. These strategies are also risk-reduction tools, enabling plan sponsors to focus more on hiring skillful managers and less on worrying about misfit risk or unintended style bets in aggregate.

Irrespective of any sort of overlay strategy, as discussed later in this chapter, bonds should range between 20% and 25% of assets. In anticipation of greater market volatility and the impact it could have on contribution levels, plan sponsors should consider a permanent allocation to either long bonds or some sort of dedicated or immunized bond portfolio specifically to cover their retired benefit obligation. As the indexed bond market grows in size and liquidity, it might also be useful as a risk-con-

---

[4]Sabine Schramm, "Index Managers Get Active" *Pensions & Investments* vol. 23 (October 16, 1995): 3.

trol vehicle for the vested benefit obligation. A plan sponsor should consider targeting 10% to 30% of the overall bond allocation to the high-yield and emerging-market bond sectors which have been growing, offering both incremental return and diversification benefits.

A permanent allocation of 15%-20% to either a passive overlay, TAA or multi-asset global manager adds greater flexibility to an institutional portfolio during periods of high market volatility and/or a high degree of portfolio restructuring activity. This chapter discusses other traditional transition management strategies employed by external transition managers, index funds, and in-house managers. Finally, it suggests that a completion fund can also serve this purpose.

Alternatives

Alternative investments such as real estate, private placements, buy-outs, or venture capital have been growing significantly and should be considered primarily by plan sponsors wishing to pursue high potential returns and some diversification benefits while not being deterred by what they are giving up in liquidity benefits. The suggested allocation of 0% to 20% will depend heavily on the funded status of the plan.

Current and projected market volatilities warrant at least considering the use of derivatives to facilitate both strategic and tactical asset allocation. The use of derivatives by plan sponsors is growing, primarily for hedging purposes. Hedging can be used not only to lock in profits but, perhaps more important, to mitigate increasing contribution levels. Current market conditions make certain hedging strategies — such as "collars" — particularly attractive.

ALLOCATION TO PASSIVE OVERLAY, TAA, AND/OR GLOBAL MULTIASSET MANAGER

Philips, Rogers, and Capaldi recently conducted a study of 11 TAA managers who collectively manage close to 95% of domestic TAA assets in the United States.[5] They broke each manager's record, net of transaction costs, into two time segments: from inception through December 1987, and from January 1988 through September 1994.

The managers demonstrated significant timing skill in the first period, corroborating an earlier study by Weigel, and little or no timing skill in the latter period. In general, TAA mangers are more challenged to add value during periods of low volatility and high correlations among asset classes. It is interesting to note that the correlation between stocks

---

[5]Thomas K. Philips, Greg T. Rogers, and Robert E. Capaldi, "Tactical Asset Allocation: 1977-1994" *Journal of Portfolio Management* vol. 23 (Fall 1996): 57.

and bonds was 0.7 in the latter period of the study, compared with 0.2 in the prior period, and that volatilities were 12% for stocks and 4% for bonds in the latter period compared with 17% and 6%, respectively, in the prior period.

If future stock market volatility remains near current levels of around 20% and if the domestic stock/bond correlation of 0.25 persists, domestic TAA should continue to be an attractive investment strategy. The most popular TAA strategies have been both quantitative and primarily "fact based." TAA processes, with at least some "forecast based" component that uses derivatives as implementation vehicles, should do better in markets with high volatility and at unprecedented valuation levels.

In general, TAA managers try to achieve better-than-benchmark returns with lower-than-benchmark volatility by forecasting the returns of two or more asset classes while systematically varying asset class exposure. Active asset allocation is designed to exploit shifts in the relative attractiveness of asset classes. Asset mix can be shifted by buying and selling the actual underlying assets in the portfolio or by buying or selling futures contracts. TAA managers can, therefore, use futures exclusively; use index funds exclusively; or use index funds primarily, but futures where practicable, to manage cash inflows and outflows on an ongoing basis.

Relatively high liquidity and low transaction costs can be achieved through the use of high volume futures markets for stocks and bonds and/or through the use of index funds. The section on traditional transition management strategies describes strategies that are often used by TAA and/or index fund managers to limit transaction costs.

Flexibility

Domestic or global TAA can add flexibility to a pension plan's asset mix. This can be extremely important if pension plans anticipate structural changes during periods of high market volatility. TAA can accomplish what plan sponsors hope to accomplish when they try to second-guess markets by "tweaking" asset allocation in the aftermath of a major market move. "Tweaking" involves not only an asset allocation but a timing decision as well. Many plan sponsors lack the resources or feel uncomfortable about making *both* of these decisions.

Under certain circumstances, TAA can also be used for transition management or until the plan sponsor finds the external manager he is hoping to hire. More often, TAA is used as an overlay strategy to rebalance to a new asset allocation, manage asset "drift," or put excess cash to work. Alternatively, plan sponsors can employ a more passive overlay approach that rebalances back to a predetermined or static mix. Using derivatives in conjunction with a passive approach provides flexibility while potentially minimizing transaction costs. Alternatively, where "crossing" is not practical, portfolio trading techniques utilizing futures to minimize transaction costs could be employed by passive — or even active strategies that typically implement asset shifts exclusively with physical assets such as index funds.

Futures Transaction Costs

Because futures volume in most markets globally exceeds stock volume, equity futures transaction costs are less than 20% of what it costs to transact in the underlying physical securities. In the United States alone, futures costs are less than 10% of what it would cost to transact in stocks. Stock trading costs include not only commissions and fees but also the marketmaker's spread and "market impact," the additional spread that might be necessary to satisfy a large trade size. Many traditional active managers who invest in individual securities find that with larger size comes less flexibility, higher transaction costs, and lower investment returns. In contrast, TAA approaches largely eliminate asset size as a deterrent to performance whenever they are able to access liquidity through the futures markets.

In addition, futures circumvent settlement differences among asset classes, which can result in nonmarket exposure for a period of time. They are also nondisruptive to the underlying asset management or to the income stream generated by those assets. Since futures reflect index returns, any overperformance or underperformance associated with the underlying assets will also stay with the portfolio.

Regarding equities, a TAA manager using futures will be buying or selling stock index futures not only to get to the target allocation but also to get to the target portfolio "beta." Similarly, on the fixed-income side, bond index futures contracts will be needed to shift to the target allocation as well as the target portfolio "duration."

Multiasset Managers

Domestic or global multiasset managers present an alternative approach to active rebalancing of a portfolio. Multiasset management that relies on security selection and asset allocation skills is probably not the most economical interim solution to transition management. Multiasset managers offer skills and research across a larger number of asset classes. They distinguish themselves by devoting resources and adding value through asset allocation and security selection. The multiasset approach makes sense for pension plans that struggle to find and implement the best asset mix at any point in time.

Since most asset allocation models contain volatility and correlation assumptions, both stock and bond index options can also be used in tactical asset allocation. An option's delta can be viewed as the component of the asset mix weight that moves with the index, circumventing the need to trade. This delta measures the rate at which option prices change with a change in stock price.

DERIVATIVES AS STRATEGIC ASSET ALLOCATION AND HEDGING TOOLS

At the end of 1995, Greenwich Associates conducted a survey of 200 pension plans to determine the extent to which derivatives were being used. Regarding equities, 40% of the respondents used index futures while 30% used options. Swaps were being used by 22 of the largest 200 U.S. pension plans. Most strategies were implemented by external money managers. Although derivatives continue to be used primarily for hedging, plan sponsors wanting to retain discretion and flexibility may consider derivatives as an alternative to facilitate both strategic and tactical asset allocation.

The following example demonstrates the use of derivatives to implement a new asset-allocation decision. Suppose a pension plan gets investment committee approval in January to increase its allocation to international equities and to fund this increase by decreasing its exposure to domestic equities. By using derivatives, such as futures or swaps, the pension plan can get the *net* exposure it wants in January.

A plan sponsor typically takes a few months to develop a comfort level with the money manager he eventually hires. When the money manager is hired, the derivatives can be exchanged for physical assets (EFP) through a portfolio trade. As discussed in the next section, converting derivatives into stock can often be carried out as a single transaction through an EFP, usually resulting in lower total execution costs.

Let's go back to January. The plan sponsor has to decide whether to trade into physical assets, use futures or swaps, or just wait until the appropriate external manager has been found. Clearly, there is an "opportunity," or waiting, cost associated with not being invested for perhaps six to nine months. The plan sponsor will need to evaluate the effect of this cost on achieving the plan's return objective and on future contribution levels. Exhibit 3 lists the advantages and disadvantages associated with using portfolio trading, futures, and swaps in the initial transaction.

Exhibit 3: Comparison of Physicals, Futures, and Swaps

	Advantages	
Trading Physicals	*Futures*	*Swaps*
Holding "desired" securities	Low trading cost	Customize maturity, currency, base port-folio
No credit risk	Rapid execution/ Liquidity	Minimize/eliminate Basis Risk; Tracking Error, Currency Mismatch, Roll Risk; Not constrained by CFTC approval — more countries exposure; Lower trading cost than stock
	Same-day settlement	

	Disadvantages	
Trading Physicals	*Futures*	*Swaps*
Costs more for frequent asset shifts	Basis Risk	Credit Risk
Settlement Differences	Tracking Error	Less liquid
	Currency mismatch	Marking at reset dates
	Roll risk	
	CFTC approval?	
	Initial Margin & Daily Marking	
	Differ in maturity by country	

When to Trade Physicals Versus Derivatives:

Vehicle	*Investment Horizon*	*Market Volatility*
Physicals	Long & build position slowly	Low
Derivatives	Short	High

Source: Nancy C. Nakovick, "Global Derivative Strategies"
IMN Symposium, St. Petersburg, Fla. (January 14-15, 1997).

If the plan sponsor intends to hire — but has not yet hired — an "active" money manager, he won't know the manager's "desired" assets. Best case: shift from domestic to international index funds as an interim solution; then, in six to nine months, into "desired" international stock.

This strategy, however, could carry higher transaction costs than initially using a futures basket to get the desired net exposure. The futures are then converted into stock in a single transaction in six to nine months. Depending on market conditions and money flows, an index fund manager who manages both domestic and international equities might be able to mitigate some of these additional costs by taking maximum advantage of "crossing" opportunities. Since a round trip in futures costs less than 20% of the same trip for stocks, futures are a more consistent vehicle for getting international exposure at lowest cost, especially for investment horizons of less than one year.

Pricing of Futures and Swaps

Relative to cash securities, an investor in futures or swaps hopes that the interest income he is earning on the underlying notional amount will at least offset what he is foregoing in dividend and stock lending income by not owning the stocks. If futures are not trading at fair value, the investor needs to take this into account in making the derivative vehicle decision. How a dealer hedges his position will determine the swap spread. Whether he uses stock and/or futures to hedge will depend on market conditions at that time. The dealer's willingness to share profits associated with stock lending and to pass through certain dividend-withholding tax advantages will also affect the swap spread. These three factors determine how competitive a dealer can be in pricing swaps relative to futures baskets or owning cash securities outright.

Tracking a Futures Basket

Using an optimizer such as the BARRA software, a futures basket of six to 10 countries can be constructed to track EAFE within an acceptable tracking error. Exhibit 4 illustrates a basket of 10 CFTC-approved futures that were designed to track EAFE within 152 basis points. It assumes that the initial futures basket trade was done on June 30, 1995, and managed for one year. The plan sponsor's profit relative to owning cash securities outright is 51 basis points. Most of the savings is in commissions or sales taxes avoided by not transacting in the underlying securities. Contributing to the 51 basis point advantage is an 8 bp cumulative net gain associated with the rolling of quarterly and monthly futures contracts.

It is important to note that this analysis reflects market conditions over a certain period of time. A similar analysis, done when futures were predominantly trading cheap relative to fair value, probably would have yielded higher profits associated with rolling contracts. For all of 1995, annual mispricing is estimated to have been a 25 basis point net

Exhibit 4: Owning EAFE Through Stock Index Futures Versus Equity Swaps

Case: Initial futures basket trade on June 30, 1995, managed for one year.

Tracking Error: 1.52

Country		Weight %	Comm BP	Dividend Yield %	Dividend Tax Benefit BP	Annual Mis-pricing* BP	Client Cost
UK	FT100	19.82	-08	4.55	68	-17	—
Germany	DAX	8.3	-50	2.10	32	27	—
Netherlands	AEX	5.87	-50	3.11	47	-29	—
Switzerland	SMI	5.38	-50	1.79	27	39	—
France	CAC	4.63	-20	2.45	0	-10	—
Spain	IBEX	3.32	-40	3.38	51	75	—
Belgium	BEL20	2.78	-40	3.78	57	-24	—
Italy	MIB30	2.44	-40	2.52	38	-170	—
Japan	NK300	40.48	-50	0.8	12	13	—
Hong Kong	HS	6.99	-50	3.42	0	88	—
EAFE-like			-39		29	8	-2
Currency Forwards							-6
Single Currency Margining							-12
Client Profit Relative to Cash Securities							51

*1995 (Near + Calendar), benefit (+)

Source: Nancy C. Nakovick, "Global Derivative Strategies"
IMN Symposium, St. Petersburg, Fla. (January 14-15, 1997).

loss. From June 1995 through June 1996, it is interesting to note that the volatility percent deviation from fair value is 25 basis points on average per month, per country. The degree of variability during this time period seems to indicate that the 8 bp gain referred to earlier would not have been with certainty.

Uncertainty is more prevalent outside the United States, where there are fewer stocks underlying the local index futures contracts. Also, dividends tend to be in "lumps" at certain times during the year, as opposed to fairly even distribution as is the case in the United States. To help plan sponsors manage through this uncertainty, they should maintain close contact with their brokers when it is time to roll contracts, particularly contacts outside the United States. Alternatively, plan sponsors could hire an external manager.

Tracking Swaps

As an alternative to the futures basket in Exhibit 4, Exhibit 5 shows the pricing of an 11 country EAFE-like swap. It assumes that the transaction is initiated on June 30, 1995 and has a one-year maturity. The tracking error is 105 basis points. The plan sponsor's profit relative to cash securities is 45 basis points or a six-point disadvantage to futures — which can be considered at the noise level.

Exhibit 5: Owning EAFE Through Stock Index Futures Versus Equity Swaps

Case: Use cash securities to hedge EAFE-like exposure except Japan, where futures are used. Swap transaction initiated on June 30, 1995 for a period of one year, yearly reset, price return only.

Tracking Error: 1.05

Country		Weight %	Commission BP	Dividend Yield %	Net Dividend Yield %	Swap Spread to Local Libor BP	Basis Swap BP	Client Profit BP
UK	FT100	19	90	4.55	5.35	-525.29	-521.15	160.29
Germany	DAX	8	35	2.10	0.00	-30.00	-30.19	65.00
Netherlands	AEX	6	40	3.11	3.11	-306.00	-308.13	35.00
Switzerland	SMI	5	40	1.79	1.79	-174.00	-176.31	35.00
France	CAC	5	60	2.45	3.12	-325.37	-324.23	183.11
Spain	IBEX	3	40	3.38	3.38	-333.00	-325.48	35.00
Belgium	BEL20	3	70	3.78	5.04	-459.00	-460.98	267.82
Italy	MIB30	2	70	2.52	2.52	-232.00	-225.55	50.00
Japan	NK300	40	46	0.80	1.00	-14.00	-14.35	-20.00
Hong Kong	HS	7	67	3.42	3.42	-202.00	-201.52	-73.00
Singapore	basket	2	100	2.70	2.70	-170.00	-172.12	0.00
EAFE-like				2.32	2.45	-197.80	-198.15	45.63

Source: Nancy C. Nakovick, "Global Derivative Strategies"
IMN Symposium, St. Petersburg, Fla. (January 14-15, 1997).

Except for Japan, where futures were used, the broker/dealer in this example hedged his position primarily with cash securities in quoting the swap spread of Libor — 198 basis points. The spreads reflects the passing through of tax benefits and stock lending profits, which more than offset whatever commissions the plan sponsor would have paid to hold cash securities. By comparing the net dividend with the dividend yield column, the plan sponsor can determine the countries where the broker/dealer has tax treaties and to what extent he has enabled the plan sponsor to share in these benefits. Except for Germany, swap pricing assumes no reinvestment of dividends.

As shown in Exhibit 6, the swap example can be expanded to include 16 of the 20 countries in EAFE as of June 30, 1995 for the same one-year maturity. The tracking error drops significantly to 55 basis points. The plan sponsor's profit relative to cash securities is 38 basis points or a 12 basis-point disadvantage to futures. In this example, the swap spread assumes no extra structuring costs above what the plan sponsor would have paid to transact in the cash securities markets of the additional five countries. Typically, a minimum investment for an EAFE-like swap is $3 million. Emerging market swaps are also possible and practical from a transaction cost/liquidity perspective.

Exhibit 6: Owning EAFE Through Stock Index Futures Versus Equity Swaps

Case: Use cash securities to hedge EAFE-like exposure except Japan, where futures are used. Swap transaction initiated on June 30, 1995 for a period of one year, yearly reset, price return only.

Tracking Error: 0.55

Country		Weight %	Com-mis-sion BP	Divi-dend Yield %	Net Divi-dend Yield %	Swap Spread to Local Libor BP	Basis Swap BP	Client Profit BP
UK	FT100	16	90	4.55	5.35	-525.29	-521.15	160.29
Germany	DAX	7	35	2.10	0.00	-30.00	-30.19	65.00
Netherlands	AEX	5	40	3.11	3.11	-306.00	-308.13	35.00
Switzerland	SMI	5	40	1.79	1.79	-174.00	-176.31	35.00
France	CAC	6	60	2.45	3.12	-325.37	-324.23	183.11
Spain	IBEX	2	40	3.38	3.38	-333.00	-325.48	35.00
Belgium	BEL20	1	70	3.78	5.04	-459.00	-460.98	267.82
Italy	MIB30	3	70	2.52	2.52	-232.00	-225.55	50.00
Japan	NK300	40	46	0.80	1.00	-14.00	-14.35	-20.00
Hong Kong	HS	4	67	3.42	3.42	-202.00	-201.52	-73.00
Singapore	basket	2	60	1.71	1.71	-111.00	-112.39	0.00
Malaysia	basket	3	100	1.65	1.65	-64.49	-64.82	0.00
Denmark	basket	1	30	1.97	1.97	-167.50	-168.82	0.00
Finland	basket	1	30	2.33	2.33	-203.30	-203.81	0.00
Sweden	basket	2	30	2.25	2.25	-195.19	-193.24	0.00
Australia	basket	3	60	4.14	4.14	-354.46	-348.92	0.00
EAFE-like		100	—	2.18	2.45	—	-183.11	38.64

Source: Nancy C. Nakovick, "Global Derivative Strategies"
IMN Symposium, St. Petersburg, Fla. (January 14-15, 1997).

TRADITIONAL TRANSITION MANAGEMENT STRATEGIES

Portfolio trading involves the buying or selling of securities as portfolios, as opposed to single securities, and tries to minimize transaction costs. Trading in multiple markets can be done simultaneously. There are three components to transaction costs: commissions; market impact; and opportunity cost, or the interim cost of being in cash and temporarily not being invested in desired securities.

Pension plans can use portfolio trading techniques to change portfolio managers, invest cash contributions, raise cash for benefit payments, or rebalance in-house portfolios. When using portfolio trading to facilitate manager transitions, plan sponsors can control the asset shift in-house, usually more profitably and often with less risk than if the managers being hired and terminated did the trading themselves. This is because the sponsor is able to aggregate buys and sells across managers to create a more diversified portfolio.

Compared with trading securities individually, a portfolio trade is more diversified and can often be hedged more economically by the broker, resulting in lower transaction costs for the plan sponsor. Alternatively, the plan sponsor can hire an external transition manager to facilitate the process.

Portfolio Trading Strategies

There are at least two, and possibly three, different ways to trade an equity portfolio. On a pure agency basis, the plan sponsor shares a list with the broker of the actual names of the stocks to be traded. The broker then trades the stocks on a best-efforts or incentive basis. Agency trading has the lowest commissions, but the *total* cost is unknown.

In a principal trade, the plan sponsor does not reveal in advance the names of the stocks to be traded. Instead, the sponsor reveals certain portfolio characteristics such as number of securities, market value, futures correlation, tracking error, liquidity, and industry distribution. Based on these characteristics, the broker/dealer quotes a price as a spread — usually off the closing value of either the portfolio or the individual stocks in the portfolio. There are several advantages to principal trading, including immediate implementation (that is, no opportunity cost) and the individual stocks are not subject to market impact. The spread, however, reflects the broker/dealer's cost to take the portfolio into inventory and immediately hedge it. Hedging costs are typically higher in more volatile markets. The broker/dealer also needs to price into the spread correlation risk to the extent that the portfolio cannot be perfectly hedged. To minimize correlation risk, nonindex stocks should be traded separately as agency, with the remaining portion of the portfolio that correlates well with hedging vehicles as principal. Factors that influence when to do a principal versus agency trade include: size of the trade, the stocks to be traded, prevailing market conditions, and the inventory position of the broker-dealer. Often, when trading agency, size and market volatility become a nonissue if the trade is "two way" or dollar-balanced between buys and sells. Capabilities that need to be evaluated in choosing an agency broker include: daily trading volume, access to multiple liquidity channels, and ability to provide real-time updates of trading opportunities.

EFP Whether the trade is done agency or principal, both EFP(exchange-for-physical) trades and basis trades draw on the liquidity of the futures markets to reduce trading costs. In an EFP, the plan sponsor may want to buy a portfolio of primarily S&P 500 stocks from the broker/dealer in exchange for S&P 500 index futures that the plan sponsor is currently holding. With an EFP, the futures are held in the name of the pension plan and are essentially traded at the close. The effective price at which stocks are actually delivered to the pension plan is a function of individual closing prices plus or minus the futures' fair-value spread off the close. The spread may also reflect the portfolio's correlation risk with the index.

Basis Trades Basis trades enable plan sponsors or their money managers who are precluded from holding any sort of derivative instruments to rebalance portfolios more economically, invest or raise cash, or facilitate transitioning managers. A basis trade is similar to an EFP except that the futures are held in the name of the broker/dealer, not the pension plan, and futures are being traded throughout the day based on the plan sponsor's or his manager's instructions. The price at which stocks are delivered is a function of individual closing prices plus or minus a weighted average spread to fair value depending on where the broker/dealer traded his equivalent futures position. The spread may also reflect the portfolio's correlation risk with the index.

STYLE MANAGEMENT
AND APPROPRIATE BENCHMARKS

To create a successful investment program, a plan sponsor needs to identify not only the individual money manager's style and skill but also his various managers' investment style in aggregate, relative to an overall asset-class benchmark. A manager's investment style can be defined in terms of a set of financial attributes or factors that have proven over time to be significantly correlated to his performance. Equity managers can be categorized in terms of criteria such as average market capitalizations, dividend or earnings yields, and earnings growth. Fixed-income managers tend to be categorized by portfolio duration or quality ratings. Looking back historically, the performance difference between domestic equity growth-and-value portfolios exceeds 10 percentage points per year in many 36-month periods. It seems improbable that any active domestic equity manager could use skill to overcome the impact of style on performance.

The Role of Benchmarks

By way of review, a benchmark is a passive, investable representation of a manager's process and security universe. A valid benchmark should be unambiguous, investable, measurable, consistent with the investment risk characteristics of the manager's portfolio, reflective of current investment opinions regarding the securities within the benchmark, and specified in advance. A benchmark portfolio, therefore, should be able to replicate a manager's style.

Evaluating Manager Skill A manager's skill can be evaluated through the use of an information ratio. It represents the ratio of a manager's returns in excess of his style benchmark divided by the variability of this excess. Skillful managers will produce high information ratios.

Although a particular style should not be expected to outperform the market consistently, a manager's investment skill should result in excess performance relative to his style benchmark whether his style is in or out of favor. After fees, particularly skillful domestic equity managers can be expected to outperform their style benchmarks by 100-200 basis points per year. A comparable degree of outperformance can be expected from superior domestic fixed-income managers relative to their specific style benchmarks.

International Aspects Internationally, where the markets are less efficient for both stocks and bonds, the degree of outperformance is greater by even median managers relative to broad market indices. In the three-year period ending June 1997, this outperformance was as much as 400-500 basis points. At this time, style can be defined internationally with much less precision than for domestic managers. Consequently, in analyzing style internationally, users need to exercise a certain degree of sophistication in interpreting the outputs from currently available software packages.

In Aggregate Individual manager benchmark portfolios play a valuable role in the creation of an efficient overall portfolio of multiple managers. In combination, they represent the overall asset-class benchmark and risk profile that the plan sponsor's managers should maintain in aggregate. A completion fund is often used, as discussed in the next section, to eliminate unintended style bias and to ensure complete market coverage. The use of a completeness fund allows the plan sponsor to focus on identifying skillful managers who can deliver a consistent performance relative to well-specified benchmarks as opposed to searching for and hiring style specific managers.

COMPLETION FUND AS A RISK REDUCTION TOOL AND MANAGER TRANSITION VEHICLE

The completion fund concept may well define money management in this decade. Plan sponsors try to identify hidden risk that can skew their returns. The risk is that the plan might deviate from its overall asset-class benchmark because of an unintended style bet created by selecting an insufficiently diverse group of managers. The solution is to fill the gaps with a completion fund. If not controlled, style risk can swamp the benefits of skillful stock selection, particularly in a multiple manager framework.

The completion fund benchmark should be set as the difference between the aggregate of all the benchmarks for a fund's active managers and the target benchmark for the overall asset class. Each manager is then judged by his stock-picking ability relative to his benchmark, while the completion fund corrects for the misfit that the sponsor created in allocating assets to particular managers. Much of the need for the completion fund comes from the use of custom benchmarks. These custom benchmarks allow a plan sponsor to measure a manager's skill without waiting for the manager's style to come full cycle.

Some plan sponsors analyze their style risk with the help of a consulting firm; others do so in-house using software such as BARRA. The analysis typically reveals unintended capitalization and/or industry biases, usually with a systematic underweighting of large-cap value stocks.

Role in Risk Reduction

Completion funds, in general, should not be looked at as vehicles to boost performance but rather to reduce misfit risk. They tend to include an odd assortment of utility, oil, and bank stocks. Some plan sponsors have shifted from a passive to an active approach to reduce trading costs and perhaps add incremental return. Active completeness funds can also facilitate manager transitions at significantly lower cost and are a viable alternative to more traditional portfolio trading techniques. Assuming that the overall portfolio of managers was in style balance prior to the firing of a manager, the fired manager's stocks would then be integrated into the completion fund, and the fund's benchmark would be modified to reflect the fired manager's style. Through the use of a completion fund, stocks can be absorbed and redistributed without incurring market-impact or commission costs. The savings are estimated to be 60% to 80% of the costs that are normally associated with selling an active manager's portfolio and reinvesting the proceeds into an index fund. Estimates for transition costs using a completion fund are in the range of 5 to 8 basis points per year, not to mention the additional benefit of reduced misfit risk of perhaps 1%-2%.

Completion funds are more often associated with domestic equities but can be applied to international equities as well. Since style analysis is not as well defined for foreign equities and managers tend not to be hired with style mandates, an international completion fund tends to focus on country risk as opposed to the sector and/or the capitalization risk of its U.S. equity counterpart.

THE ETERNAL QUEST FOR ALPHA

Market-neutral or a long/short strategy allows the investor to separate security selection from the asset allocation decision. The basic principle is to invest in one or more mispriced securities and to hedge out the market risk. The following strategies are considered market-neutral:

- Merger arbitrage   Long   stock of company being acquired
     Short   stock of acquiring company
- Long/Short
  equity portfolios   Long   a basket of undervalued stocks
     Short   a basket of overvalued stocks in the same market
- Convertible   Long   cheap convertible bond
  bond hedging   Short   underlying stock with the same net exposure
- Bond-basis hedging   Long   (short) bond future
     Short   (long) underlying bond
- Different share   Long   (short) ordinary share
  classes   Short   (long) nonvoting share
- Mortgage hedging   Long   mortgages
     Short   equivalent duration exposure

- Tight yield-curve   Long   (short) 5-year government bond
  trading   Short   (long) 7-year government bond
                       Long   (short) 9-year government bond
                               with net zero duration.

Strategies that are not market neutral:

- Long/short currencies   Long   one currency
                                 Short   another currency in
                                         equivalent dollar
                                         amount
- Spreads outside of directly   Long   one market (equity or
  related markets   fixed income)
                                 Short   another market (equity
                                         or fixed income)
- General yield-curve trading   Long   (short) 20-year bond
                                 Short   (long) Treasury bill.[6]

Long/short is not without risk, but the risk can be controlled. The key to controlling risk is the balance between the long and short positions. For example, a plan sponsor might have $10 million to invest. Of this total, $1 million would be set aside as a liquidity buffer, with $9 million available to invest as $9 million in long and $9 million in short positions. In the case of equity portfolios, risk can be reduced significantly if the offsetting positions are evenly balanced with respect not only to dollar volume but also industry group and company capitalization.

Prior to the January 1995 IRS ruling, plan sponsors were concerned that borrowing stock to initiate a short sale would create a taxable event. As a result of this ruling, buying stock on margin can result in unrelated business taxable income, but a short sale alone will not. The various market-neutral styles tend to be uncorrelated and can vary in terms of degree of leverage and portfolio composition. Some plan sponsors may find that a diversified portfolio of market-neutral styles can add value while reducing the risk to any individual manager or style.

In contrast, a typical hedge fund manager given $10 million to invest by a plan sponsor might choose to use leverage to buy shares valued at $12 million and to sell short shares valued at $6 million. His gross investment is therefore $18 million, or 180% of the plan sponsor's initial

---

[6]Jane Buchen, "Diversifying Market-Neutral Strategies" *Market Neutral: State-of-the-Art Strategies for Every Market Environment*, edited by Jess Lederman and Robert A. Klein, Irwin Professional Publishers. (Chicago: 1996).

investment. The net exposure is only $6 million ($12 million long/$6 million short). The portfolio is biased toward a long exposure, so it is described as being 60% net long ($6 million net exposure/$10 million initial investment). Unlike the long/short strategy in the previous paragraph, the use of leverage by the hedge fund could trigger unrelated business taxable income which is payable on all gains attributable to this use of leverage. However, if the same pension fund invests in a qualified offshore fund, there is no UBTI payable.

Not all hedge funds can be characterized as market neutral, but those that are can also vary in terms of degree of leverage and portfolio composition. Plan sponsors considering investing in hedge funds should construct a diversified portfolio of uncorrelated funds and styles. Because of the risks in hedge fund investing, the use of a knowledgeable industry adviser is highly recommended.

High-Yield Asset Class

Offering both incremental return and diversification benefits, high yield is a hybrid asset class behaving more like bonds or stocks depending on market circumstances. Prices react to interest rate movements but to a lesser extent than traditional fixed income securities. Credit quality and the credit outlook have a greater impact. High yield should perform better in periods of economic expansion even though interest rates may be increasing.

Performance is linked to narrowing credit spreads, reflecting a more favorable operating environment for the issuing company. Conversely, credit implications may cause high yield to underperform in a recessionary environment, but this underperformance will be somewhat mitigated by the decline in interest rates.

Historically, high-yield securities have more than adequately compensated investors when measured in terms of excess return per unit of risk. In fact, historical performance data suggest that an allocation to high yield would have enhanced returns without increasing volatility in either a fixed-income or balanced portfolio. Plan sponsors should consider targeting approximately 20% of the fixed-income allocation to high yield.

Allocation of 10% to 20% to high-yield historically has not resulted in an unacceptable lowering of a plan sponsor's aggregated fixed-income portfolio's overall credit quality. Since high yield is one of the most research-intensive fixed-income sectors, value-added research can contribute significantly to any given manager's performance. According to *P&I*, noninvestment-grade bonds experienced a 34% increase to $6.541 billion for the year ending September 20, 1996, in part, due to a particularly strong performance.[8]

Real Estate Activity

Many U.S. pension plans continue to increase their domestic commercial real estate activity in anticipation of stable to higher returns for real estate going forward while lower returns are expected for financial instruments. They are expanding their allocations to take advantage of newer options such as opportunity funds, real estate investment trusts, and, to some extent, commercial mortgage-backed securities.

Strategic alliances are being formed with their managers. The managers are expected to have an understanding of the plan sponsor's total real estate portfolio and to make investments accordingly. According to *P&I*, real estate equity investments by the 200 leading defined benefit plans increased by 26% to $64.7 billion in the year ending September 20,1996. Assets in private equity and buyouts rose by 54% to $25.55 billion due to a strong returns and increased allocations. Venture capital rose 51% to $10.65 billion while private debt decreased marginally. The 200 leading DB plans reported the following percent allocations for: private equity to 19% from 15%; buyout funds to 16% from 10.5%; venture capital to 43% from 35.5%.[7]

CONCLUSION

Although the funded status of public pension plans has been improving steadily since 1984, contributions have not always kept pace with liabilities due to:

- Political pressures to award benefit increases.
- Lackluster asset performance due to suboptimal asset mixes.
- A low interest rate environment (current and projected).
- Increasing volatility in the capital markets.[8]

This chapter has suggested strategies that could potentially provide faster, more prudent asset growth to help plan sponsors meet future obligations. It has also discussed briefly how derivative strategies can help plan sponsors manage through current and projected market volatility. Finally, several strategies using both internal and external managers have been delineated to enable plan sponsors to make a more economical transition between asset classes, styles, and/or managers.

---

[7]Marlene G. Starr, "Real Estate Equity Assets Rise 26%" *Pensions & Investments* vol. 25 (January 20, 1997): 22.

[8]Marlene G. Starr, op. cit.

Christopher E. D'Amore is a principal of State Street Global Advisors, which he joined in 1987. D'Amore is a portfolio manager for global active equity strategies and is actively involved in product development, marketing, and client service.

From 1993 through November 1995 he was director of structured portfolio management and operations for State Street Global Advisors, Canada, Ltd., where he managed all Canadian client index funds and global derivative products. Earlier in his career at SSgA, D'Amore's responsibilities included management of the international common trust funds and U.S. equity index funds. He also served as a manager in SSgA's international operations area.

D'Amore holds a bachelor of arts degree in business from Ohio University and a master's degree in business administration from Suffolk University.

Joshua G. Feuerman, CFA, is a principal of State Street Global Advisors who also joined the company in 1987. Feuerman is a manager of both developed and emerging markets portfolios in SSgA's global equities group. He also assists in the marketing of SSgA's equity products to existing and prospective clients as well as to the consultant community.

Earlier at SSgA, Feuerman was responsible for research and development in the active international equities group.

He holds a bachelor of arts degree in economics and Romance languages from Bowdoin College and a master's degree in business administration, in finance, from the University of Chicago. Feuerman is an adjunct lecturer in economics at Brandeis University.

Chapter 6

Investing Pension Assets in International Equities

Christopher E. D'Amore
Principal
State Street Global Advisors

Joshua G. Feuerman, CFA
Principal
State Street Global Advisors

While the waters of international investing are not considered uncharted, to many plan sponsors the topic is — pardon the pun — foreign. This chapter will help to unravel some of the mysteries and misconceptions of investing public pension funds outside the United States. The first section addresses the case for investing internationally. We explain how international equities provide the means to reduce a U.S. public fund's risk by expanding the opportunity set of investments. The reasons why it is not prudent to put all one's money into one U.S. stock are the same reasons why one should invest abroad.

The second section answers the question: Can a public fund get international diversification by holding U.S. companies doing business abroad? While many plan sponsors understand the benefits of diversification, they believe they can obtain these benefits by owning shares of multinationals such as Coca-Cola and Gillette. Intuitively, this strategy might seem to make sense. In reality, however, international diversification requires a different approach.

The final section tackles the Japan issue and how much Japanese equity exposure a public fund should have in its portfolio. Japan is always a hot topic because it plays a large role in most international portfolios, and investors have been struggling with the Japanese equity issue since the first dollar was converted into yen. We provide some information to help investors reach a conclusion on Japanese equity exposure.

This chapter just scratches the surface of international investing. Our goal is to provide facts and figures to help sponsors answer some of the many questions surrounding international equities. In other words, we are trying to make international investing somewhat less foreign and help plan sponsors navigate the waters to reach their long-term investment objectives.

WHY INTERNATIONAL?

This section explores the rationale for investing outside the U.S. market. It presents statistics to demonstrate the opportunities and benefits of strategic overseas investing. We will look at the role the United States plays in the global economy and how that role has changed over recent decades. We will also provide data on the substantial movement of capital outside of the United States.

Go Global

For the past decade, investors have been hearing the advice, go global, from consultants and investment managers alike. With U.S. investors riding one of the most robust bull markets in history, why consider international equities?

The U.S. stock market has produced substantial returns over the last decade and incredible returns over the past few years. Why would U.S. investors, enjoying the benefits of an open market with low transaction costs and high liquidity, need to go anywhere else?

The question becomes even more difficult to answer in light of the relatively dismal performance of foreign markets over the past few years, as represented by the Morgan Stanley Capital International Europe, Australia, and the Far East (MSCI EAFE) Index.

The answer, ironically, is simple. Investing globally substantially increases the opportunity set of investment alternatives. This increased opportunity set will diversify a portfolio, thereby lowering its overall risk. The U.S. market, arguably the most diversified and extensive in the world, is, however, just what its name implies: a single market linked to a single financial system and economy.

Even with the extensive global trade and economic links the United States maintains, it is driven primarily by internal influences which affect the market as a whole. At the end of the trading day, a fund that has invested only in the U.S. market has made a single, concentrated bet on one market — and nothing more.

By extending exposure to international markets, plan sponsors tap into the power of portfolio diversification. The addition of uncorrelated assets will significantly lower the risk of the portfolio from its previous level of being invested solely in U.S. stocks.

The Attractions of Home

It is easy to understand why investors find the U.S. market so attractive. It is highly liquid and provides a broad base of well-diversified companies that, within their respective industries, might appear to be the largest in the world. Upon closer examination, however, we found that U.S. companies may not be as large as investors assume. We looked at the top five companies around the world, as measured by total sales revenue, in four industries: electronics, retail, life insurance, and utilities. As shown in Exhibit 1, we found that U.S. companies no longer rank among the top five in electronics or utilities; they maintain only two of the top five rankings among retailers and only one of the top five within life insurance.

Exhibit 1: Largest Companies by Industry

Electronics		*Life Insurance (Stock)*	
1. Hitachi	Japan	1. Allianz Holding	Germany
2. Siemens	Germany	2. UAP*	France
3. Toshiba	Japan	3. Zurich Versicherun	Switzerland
4. NEC Corp.	Japan	4. American Int'l Group	U.S.A.
5. Alcatel	France	5. Assic Generali, spa	Italy
Specialist Retailers		*Utilities*	
1. WalMart Stores	U.S.	1. Veba AG	Germany
2. Metro AG	Germany	2. Tokyo Electric Power	Japan
3. Sears Roebuck & Co.	U.S.	3. RWE AG	Germany
4. Kmart Corp.	U.S.	4. Viag AG	Germany
5. Carrefour	France	5. Kansai Electric Power	Japan

It is clear that, for shares representing these industries, public funds seeking large, well-established companies should begin to look outside of the United States. The top five rankings, while interesting, are not very useful unless one is looking only at those specific industries.

Total Capitalization

What happens if we take a broader look at the global capital equity market? The best way to look at the overall size a country represents, and hence the aggregate opportunity, is to look at its total capitalization. In 1970, the United States represented over 66% of the world on the global equity markets' total capitalization. Clearly, this is a compelling argument for not straying too far from home. By 1996, however, the United States represented only 40% of the total. Even more interesting is the fact that this 40% reflects the stupendous relative return of the U.S. market in 1995 and 1996. So, an investor who is looking to expand his investment universe is able to capture only 40% of the world's opportunities by remaining solely in the U.S. market.

Over the last few years, plan sponsors who did not heed the call to go global are quick to point out the dismal performance of EAFE which, indeed, has left much to be desired. This record of performance would seem to indicate that the United States was the place to be invested. However, this attitude is very time-specific and short-term in nature.

What should matter to investors, especially public funds, is long-term results. Although short-term results for EAFE look bad, the picture changes dramatically over a longer period. If we look at returns beginning in 1960, we see that the U.S. market has produced a compounded annual rate of return of 11.1%. During the same period, non-U.S. equities have produced a 12.8% return. This comparison indicates that the opportunity to capitalize on investment return exists in both arenas.

Correlation of Assets

Can a public fund gain from including international investments in its portfolio? Adding international assets to a fund is effective because returns on foreign stocks and U.S. stocks are not highly correlated. Therefore, their relative return streams will not be highly correlated as well. Assets with low correlations, those that tend not to rise and fall together, will have offsetting effects on the total portfolio return, therefore dampening the overall volatility (risk) of the portfolio.

Correlation of assets can range from 1.0 to –1.0. Assets with a correlation of 1.0 are perfectly correlated and will move exactly in tandem. Assets with a correlation of –1.0 are perfectly uncorrelated and will move exactly opposite one another. The lower the correlation, the greater the diversification benefit.

Compare EAFE and the Russell 3000 Index from 1979 to 1996. The correlation is 0.45, meaning that as one asset moves, it will be followed only partially by the other. So when investors are faced with deteriorating returns in the U.S. market, they may be faced with improving returns in the international markets. A combination of low-correlation assets allows public funds to achieve their return objectives by investing in non-U.S. equities while simultaneously diversifying the portfolio.

Risk Diversification

It has long since been proven that the more diversified a portfolio, the less risky. Adding international markets to a portfolio is no exception. Although more volatile on their own, as evidenced by the higher standard deviation of returns (17.3% for EAFE versus 14.5% for the S&P 500 from 1979 to March 1997), the addition of international markets has the potential to lower the standard deviation of an overall portfolio. If we look at the risk/return tradeoff of allocating a portion of assets to non-U.S. markets, we see more compelling evidence. Ten-year rolling periods from 1975 to 1996 show that in all periods adding international exposure lowers the portfolio's risk. As shown in Exhibit 2, allocations as low as 10% can have a dramatic impact on the overall risk of a portfolio.

Exhibit 2: Risk/Return Analysis
10 Years Ending 1996

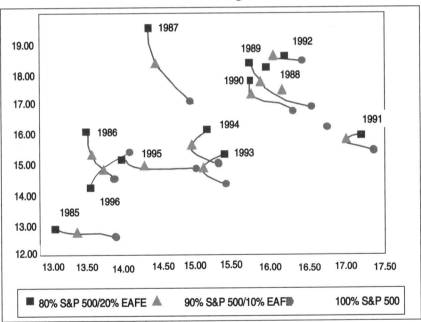

Currency Fluctuation

Whenever investors move assets outside their home market, they take on the additional risk of currency fluctuation. Investing internationally imparts an extra source of uncertainty relative to the domestic asset.

Currency risk is a concern for investors, because large adverse swings in currency values could eliminate any positive returns gained from investing abroad. Sponsors concerned with foreign currency exposure may plan on reducing or eliminating this risk by hedging currency exposure back into U.S. dollars. Even on a fully hedged basis, international investments still provide diversification benefits similar to unhedged. The correlation of the EAFE-Hedged index and Russell 3000 is 0.56.

The debate on whether to invest outside of the United States is ongoing. Yet statistics support the global concept. Are investors in the United States moving assets overseas? The answer is a resounding yes. The amount of U.S. tax-exempt assets invested overseas in 1996 has increased over 500% since 1989. Even more dramatic are estimates looking forward to 2001, by which time the number is expected to double again from the 1996 level.

What is the source of this money? While it is true that most of the money has come from corporate pension funds, public funds have been growing and are expected to catch up very soon. By the year 2001, the gap will narrow considerably between U.S. tax-exempt private and public funds invested outside of the United States. Highlighting this shift is the growth in retail funds invested outside of the United States. The growth is dramatic in both fund options available and assets invested since 1987.

Today more than ever, U.S. public funds are beginning to think globally. They have grasped the tremendous opportunities and the risk-reduction benefits that exist in foreign equity markets. Although the U.S. market may be very attractive, plan sponsors have come to realize that it is just one of many markets in the global opportunity set.

CAN I SHOP AT HOME?

The Economist publishes a Big Mac index, which shows the cost of McDonald's famous burger in cities around the world. The Big Mac index shows the relative cost of goods among countries, and also serves as a predictor of future currency movements (to even out the cost differentials). Moreover, it begs the question: If McDonald's, a U.S.-based company, is in Zurich, Sydney, Beijing, and Moscow, why do I have to invest in companies based in those countries? Another way to ask this question is: Do I have to invest internationally? The best reason to invest internationally is to gain risk diversification, which reduces the overall volatility of a portfolio. While many plan sponsors embrace the concept of international diversification, they believe they can gain this diversification by holding a basket of U.S. companies that sell their products internationally.

The reasoning goes as follows: If the majority of a company's sales occur overseas, then the company's earnings and stock price should move up and down with changes in the economies of the countries where they are doing business. A U.S. fund buying a portfolio of these multinational companies could therefore diversify a U.S. stock portfolio without having to stray from the U.S. market.

International Sales Screens

In reality, things just don't work this way. We looked at a universe of 6,000 U.S. companies from January 1990 through December 1996 to find those with a majority of sales each year coming from outside the United States. We sorted the companies into four groups, comprising companies with 60%, 70%, 80%, and 90% of their sales generated from outside the United States. While not many companies passed the screen at the higher levels, a good number passed the 60% screen, as shown in Exhibit 3.

Exhibit 3: Companies that Passed the International

% of Sales from Outside the U.S.	Number of Companies
60	35
70	19
80	9
90	6

After grouping the companies according to the percentage of sales from outside the United States, we looked at three portfolio construction techniques for each group: equal weighted, cap weighted and foreign sales weighted. For each portfolio construction method, we calculated the correlation between the portfolio and the S&P 500, and the portfolio and EAFE. Exhibits 4 through 7 show the results by group. For comparison purposes, the correlation between the S&P 500 and EAFE over this time period was 0.45.

The results show that one cannot obtain the benefits of international diversification by investing solely in U.S. multinationals. Only limiting the universe to companies for which 80% or 90% of sales come from outside the United States will generate correlations close to the correlation of the S&P 500 and EAFE. If an investor were comfortable with the slightly higher correlation of the 80% portfolio, the small number of companies that meet this criterion would limit the feasibility. There were

Exhibit 4: Companies with 60% or More
Of International Sales

Construction Methodology	Correlation with S&P 500	Correlation with EAFE
Equal Weighted	0.83	0.52
Cap Weighted	0.79	0.50
Sales Weighted	0.69	0.50

Exhibit 5: Companies with 70% or More
Of International Sales

Construction Methodology	Correlation with S&P 500	Correlation with EAFE
Equal Weighted	0.72	0.58
Cap Weighted	0.63	0.54
Sales Weighted	0.59	0.56

Exhibit 6: Companies with 80% or More
Of International Sales

Construction Methodology	Correlation with S&P 500	Correlation with EAFE
Equal Weighted	0.54	0.45
Cap Weighted	0.56	0.51
Sales Weighted	0.53	0.51

Exhibit 7: Companies with 90% or More
Of International Sales

Construction Methodology	Correlation with S&P 500	Correlation with EAFE
Equal Weighted	0.37	0.33
Cap Weighted	0.38	0.26
Sales Weighted	0.32	0.36

nine companies that passed this screen, and their average daily volume is $2.8 million. This means that if an investor were comfortable holding five days worth of a security's trading volume, this strategy could be implemented with no more than $125 million.

The hidden jewel is the 90%-or-better group, which is actually a more effective diversifier than EAFE. However, with only six names in the portfolio and an average daily volume of $400,000, this strategy would be limited to a $12 million allocation at best. The main problem with trying to implement these strategies is that the investor may turn out to be his own worst enemy. If you hold, or attempt to hold, substantial positions in a security, you may experience or create large market impact. When you try to buy the stock, you may bid the price up, and when you try to sell you may force the price down.

The Country Influence

The theory of investing in multinational companies to gain the diversification benefits of international investing does not hold water. One reason is that while stock returns are determined by company-specific factors, there is an additional country influence in stock returns. This position would argue that even if Coca-Cola derives a majority of its sales from outside of the United States, its stock will still move up and down with changes in the U.S. stock market.

A more likely explanation is that companies have been more efficient and effective in hedging their exposures to non-U.S. revenue sources. International diversification comes through exposure to the foreign equity markets and currencies. If a multinational company were able to hedge away its currency exposure, investors in the company would lose their exposure to these currencies. For example, if McDonald's can estimate its exposure to the Swiss franc, it can hedge this exposure away through the currency market. By hedging the currency risk away, the McDonald's in Zurich, Liverpool, or Acapulco is not that different from the McDonald's in Boston or Bismarck.

One final possible explanation is that the companies that make up these portfolios tend to be household names. The idea behind investing internationally is that countries go through differing economic cycles at differing times, causing their stock markets to rise and fall, and this provides the diversification benefits. The portfolio of U.S. multinationals contains many household names (Exxon, Coca-Cola, IBM, for example), which people hold in good times and bad. If these companies make products that are viewed as necessities, then demand will be constant and will not change with changing economic fortunes. Additionally, multinational companies tend to be large, capital-intensive industries such as oil, banking, or automobiles. By owning just multinationals, an investor may have a systematic bias against more indigenous industries such as cement, brewing, or utilities. There are many possible explanations for why multinationals do not provide the diversification benefits that international investing offers. Like many investing ideas, the theory was good but it did not work in practice.

Most plan sponsors hear and believe the case for diversifying their funds to reduce overall risk. Carrying this further, international diversification helps reduce overall portfolio volatility, but you cannot acquire international diversification by shopping at home. In order to get these benefits, you must have a portfolio of companies that not only sell outside the United States, but are also based outside the U.S.

WHAT ABOUT JAPAN?

How much weight should Japan have in an international benchmark? This question turns out to be beside the point. In a capitalization-weighted benchmark, Japan's weight has ranged from a high of almost 65% (February 1989) to a low of almost 29% (March 1997). On average, Japan's weight has been about 35% and many plan sponsors have expressed concerns about having over one-third of their international exposure in any one country. Additionally, given Japan's more recent underperformance, many funds have been feeling the pain associated with a large exposure to Japan.

The concern about Japan's relative weight is not new. The use of gross domestic product (GDP) to determine strategic country weights was a direct result of the Japan issue. By using GDP, Japan's weight in the portfolio decreased while the weight in corresponding European equity markets went up. Investors have been struggling with this issue for some time and there are multiple ways to evaluate it. We assessed first the Japan impact on an international mandate, then the impact at the entire portfolio level.

Returns from a Developed Market

Sponsors invest internationally to diversify the risk of their portfolios. Some sponsors expect to receive higher returns for investing internationally, but there is no reason to believe that any developed market will outperform another market over extended periods of time. In other words, one should not expect a higher or lower return from Japan, Germany, Austria, etc. just because each country has a different language or a different currency.

Exhibit 8 shows the annualized returns for the capitalization-weighted benchmark MSCI EAFE, MSCI EAFE ex-Japan, and MSCI Japan going back to January of 1970.

Exhibit 8: Annualized Returns Ending March 1997

Time Period (Years)	EAFE (%)	EAFE ex-Japan (%)	Japan (%)
26.25	12.7	12.5	14.9
10	8.8	11.8	–1.9
5	12.5	15.4	4.4
3	6.8	16.4	–8.9

Japan Market Volatility

Over more than 25 years, there has not been a significant difference in returns including or excluding Japan. Over the more recent time periods, having exposure to Japan has obviously hurt returns. But, as mentioned earlier, we should not be looking to the developed international markets as a source of value added; rather, investments in these markets should be viewed as a means of reducing risk through diversification. Exhibit 9 shows the volatility, as measured by standard deviation, of EAFE, EAFE ex-Japan, and Japan over the same time periods. Volatility, like return measures, is very time-specific and the resulting conclusions would not be vastly different from those drawn from Exhibit 8.

Exhibit 9: Volatility — Annualized Standard Deviations Ending March 1997

Time Period (Years)	EAFE (%)	EAFE ex-Japan (%)	Japan (%)
26.25	17.0	16.5	22.8
10	18.0	15.7	25.2
5	13.7	11.3	22.9
3	9.9	9.0	17.1

Over extended periods of time, the volatility of the international benchmark is not greatly impacted by Japan's inclusion or exclusion. International investing reduces risk by adding an asset class that has a low correlation to the existing assets in the portfolio. Exhibit 12 shows the correlations of EAFE, EAFE ex-Japan, and Japan relative to the S&P 500.

The results in Exhibit 10 show that Japan is a very good risk diversifier for a U.S. stock portfolio. The exclusion of Japan increases the correlation with the S&P 500, thereby increasing the risk of the overall portfolio.

Exhibit 10: Correlations with S&P 500 Ending March 1997

Time Period (Years)	EAFE	EAFE ex-Japan	Japan
26.25	0.46	0.58	0.25
10	0.44	0.68	0.20
5	0.25	0.47	0.03
3	0.36	0.55	0.12

Impact on Overall Portfolio

Regarding an international allocation, changing the weight of Japan within the index potentially may impact both the risk and return of the international component. If a plan sponsor has specific reasons to believe that going forward Japan will substantially underperform the other international markets or that Japan's risk profile has changed, he should take advantage of this knowledge and alter Japan's weight. Without the belief regarding a long-term change, plan sponsors should take advantage of Japan's diversification properties within an international benchmark.

Very few U.S. investors have portfolios consisting solely of international stocks. Since we hold U.S. stocks and bonds in addition to international stocks, we need to address the Japan issue in light of its impact on the overall portfolio risk and return characteristics. Using a 60% equity/40% fixed-income allocation, we varied the international component of the 60% equities from 10% to 60%. For each portfolio, we tested Japan weights ranging from 0% of the international allocation to 60% over a 27-year period.

In terms of overall portfolio volatility, the percentage of the international exposure invested in Japan does not have any real impact until total international exposure reaches 50% of the total portfolio. At levels below 50%, the Japan exposure does not have a material impact on the portfolio's standard deviation, as shown in Exhibit 11.

Exhibit 11: Total Portfolio Annualized Standard Deviation with Varying Percentages in International and Japan Weight, Over 27 Years

% of Total Exposure in International	Japan's % of International Component				
	0	15	30	45	60
10	8.66	8.60	8.55	8.51	8.49
20	9.41	9.30	9.23	9.19	9.20
30	9.42	9.25	9.17	9.18	9.28
40	9.64	9.25	9.36	9.45	9.71
50	10.07	9.81	9.78	9.99	10.42
60	10.68	10.38	10.40	10.75	11.39

While we have focused primarily on the risk aspect of Japanese exposure, Japan's impact on portfolio returns is similar to its impact on risk. Long term, the overall impact is negligible on returns from varying Japan's weight. Exhibit 12 shows the impact on returns from varying Japan's weight in a static portfolio comprising 40% U.S. equity, 40% U.S. bonds, 20% non-U.S. equity.

Exhibit 12: Japan's Non-U.S. Exposure Annualized Returns

Time Period	0%	15%	30%	45%	60%
Jan 70 - Dec 96	11.4%	11.6%	11.7%	11.8%	11.9%
Jan 77 - Dec 96	13.0%	13.0%	13.0%	13.0%	13.0%
Jan 87 - Dec 96	12.1%	11.9%	11.7%	11.5%	11.3%
Jan 90 - Dec 96	11.5%	11.1%	10.6%	10.2%	9.7%

It is only during the most recent seven-year period that changing the Japan weight has any significant impact on returns. Over extended time periods, varying Japan's weight has a minor influence on the overall portfolio's return.

Japan is a large part of the capitalization-weighted benchmark. Changing its weight will have a large impact on both the risk and return of the non-U.S. portion of a fund but little impact on the fund's overall risk and return. From a U.S. plan sponsor's standpoint, Japan is a good diversifier of the portfolio's overall risk. Sponsors should change Japan's weight only if they believe Japan will underperform the other market for an extended period of time or if they are overly sensitive to the volatility of their non-U.S. investments.

CONCLUSION

Investment assets are now moving overseas at a greater rate than ever before. The primary reasons for this growth are the expanded opportunities that exist outside the United States, the potential for increased returns, and the reduction of risk to the overall portfolio. While the issues surrounding international investing are many and complex, the benefits can be simple: Portfolio diversification means lower volatility. Institutional investors, especially public funds, should heed these signs and move toward building a portfolio that can capture these benefits.

Joseph A. Braccia, CFA, is a vice president at Miller Anderson & Sherrerd, LLP/Morgan Stanley Asset Management.

Previously, he served as the director of public markets for the Pennsylvania State Employes' Retirement System in Harrisburg, PA. He has also served as an asset/liability manager, portfolio manager, and securities trader within the banking industry.

Braccia is a Maxima Cum Laude graduate of La Salle University, and a member of both the Financial Analysts of Philadelphia and the International Society of Financial Analysts. His work has been published in both the *Journal of Portfolio Management* and in the book, *Pension Fund Investment Management*.

Chapter 7

Strategic Currency Management
For U.S. Pension Funds

Joseph A. Braccia, CFA
Vice President
Miller Anderson & Sherrerd, LLP/
Morgan Stanley Asset Management

Since the early 1980s, U.S. pension funds have discovered the theoretical and practical benefits of adding international investments to their portfolios. Largely, this globalization movement was based upon the premise that the diversification benefits derived from an international exposure can reduce the volatility of total pension fund returns. Moreover, these international investments were expected to generate total returns comparable to those available in the domestic stock and bond markets over a long time horizon.

This argument has obvious theoretical merit, and has been widely accepted by the pension fund community. A survey conducted by Greenwich Associates, a consulting firm to the investment management profession, illustrates the extent to which this theory has been put into practice among U.S. tax-exempt investors. From 1984 to 1995, international stock investments by U.S. tax-exempt investors increased from $27 billion to $257 billion. While figures for international bond investments were not available until 1992, from that year to 1995 international bond investments increased from $30 billion to $49 billion.[1]

This same Greenwich Associates survey also indicated that U.S. tax-exempt investors plan to increase their international investment allocations. For example, by 1998 international stock investments are expected to total $390 billion, while international bond investments should grow to $65 billion.[2] Should these targets be reached, international investments would constitute more than 13% of the typical U.S. tax-exempt investor's asset allocation, which is in stark contrast to the smaller "single digit" percentage allocations typically made by these same investors just a decade ago.

---

[1]Greenwich Associates, "Investment Management 1996."
[2]*Ibid.*

There is an obvious advantage in having a portfolio diversified across countries; just as a two-stock portfolio can have a lower standard deviation of returns than a one-stock portfolio, it is also true that a two-country portfolio can have a lower standard deviation of returns than a one-country portfolio. While this argument is intuitively compelling, U.S. plan sponsors must simultaneously adopt an attitude toward risk assessment that increases the potential to capture the benefits of international investing. An awareness of the potential risks associated with international investing is essential, and these risks — which cover areas as diverse as tax implications to cultural issues — have been well documented in other publications. Despite the heightened awareness of risk in recent years, one of the most important risks associated with international investments is often minimized or overlooked — the effects of currency movements on international return patterns.

CURRENCY RISK

The typical international stock or bond is denominated in the issuer's local currency. Thus, every international investment is actually a "package" comprising two distinct components: (1) the local return on the international stock or bond investment itself (i.e., what a German investor would receive on a Deutschemark-denominated investment in a German security) and (2) the currency return resulting from the change in value of the local currency versus the U.S. dollar.[3] To a large extent, U.S. investors with international commitments have focused on the first part of this package (i.e., the local return of the stock or bond itself) while tending to ignore the powerful effects — and risks — associated with currency fluctuations. This risk is most apparent when the favorable effects of astute country and/or security selection within an international portfolio are mitigated or overwhelmed by adverse currency movements (i.e., a decline in the value of the foreign currency versus the U.S. dollar).

Through the early 1990s, U.S. plan sponsors with international exposure paid insufficient attention to the effects of currency movements; for these unhedged investors, however, ignorance proved to be bliss. Concurrent with the staggering growth in international allocations in the late 1980s and early 1990s, U.S.-based investors generally benefited from the decline in the value of the U.S. dollar, allowing U.S.-based

---

[3]Jess Lederman and Robert A. Klein, *Financial Engineering with Derivatives* (Burr Ridge, IL: Irwin, 1995). Chapter 4 of this book, which was contributed by two investment professionals at BZW Barclays Global Investors, uses this analogy to describe the currency exposure associated with international investments.

investors to translate their yen, Deutschemarks, etc., into a larger amount of "cheaper" U.S. dollars. As a result, ignorance of the potential effects of currency fluctuations on total return patterns was actually rewarded. This phenomenon is illustrated by comparing currency-hedged and unhedged international stock returns from a passive investment in the Morgan Stanley Capital International (MSCI) Europe, Australia, and Far East (EAFE) stock index.

For international stocks, the annualized total return on the MSCI EAFE Index on an unhedged basis from 1986 to 1995 was 14%. The corresponding total return on a fully-hedged basis was 8.7%.[4] Thus, the unhedged international stock strategy was far superior to the hedged strategy from 1986 through 1995. This unusual and highly time-period dependent situation has led many U.S. investors to take a sanguine view toward currency risk. The question, however, is whether once-placid U.S. based pension funds can continue to ignore the risks posed to their international portfolios stemming from currency exposure. In an era of heightened awareness of risk and risk-control, the answer appears to be no. With vast amounts of institutional assets flowing into the international arena, the topic of currency hedging takes on great significance, and certainly ranks as one of the most challenging and important issues confronting plan sponsors. This issue needs to be addressed strategically by U.S.-based investors with international commitments as a part of their overall asset allocation strategy.

HEDGING

Before delving into currency hedging, a brief primer regarding the concept of hedging is in order. In a generic context, hedging has been defined as executing a transaction that offsets an otherwise risky underlying position.[5] To the extent that the hedge is successful, the risk inherent in the underlying position can be reduced. Ideally, the instrument used for hedging purposes should have a reliable relationship to the hedger's underlying position; for investors, the underlying position would be a portfolio of securities.

When applied in an appropriate context, hedging is geared toward accomplishing risk reduction, and is classified as a risk management technique. Hedging is often inadvertently confused with speculation because both strategies tend to use some similar instruments (such as

---

[4]Data obtained from Morgan Stanley Capital International.

[5]William F. Sharpe and Gordon J. Alexander, *Investments* (4th ed.) (Englewood Cliffs: Prentice-Hall, 1990).

futures, forwards, and options), albeit for far different reasons. Speculators execute transactions in expectation of unwinding them to produce quick profits, and without regard as to whether they have an underlying position or a need for the asset in question.[6] Because of these differences, it can be said that a speculator seeks to *create* risk, while a hedger seeks to *reduce* risk. This should not be misconstrued as an attack on speculative activities, but is instead an effort to illustrate the material differences between legitimate hedging activities and outright speculation.

Therefore, hedging can be thought of as a form of insurance, and just like all forms of insurance it is not free. Costs associated with hedging typically include transactions costs, management fees, and opportunity costs. As is always the case, a prospective hedger must evaluate the cost of entering into and maintaining a hedge versus the hedge's potential risk-reduction benefits.

CURRENCY HEDGING

If one can appreciate the purpose of hedging in general, then it becomes clear that currency hedging is merely a specialized form of hedging. A currency hedger enters into a transaction that offsets the inherent currency risk of an underlying position. For practical purposes, the underlying position is likely to be composed almost exclusively of international stock and bond investments denominated in foreign currencies. Currency risk arises from the volatility of portfolio returns due to fluctuating exchange rates. To reduce or mitigate this risk, a currency hedge can be established.

Currency futures, currency options, and currency forward contracts can be used as a part of the hedging program to reduce the volatility of total return patterns and protect the value of an international investment program against adverse currency movements. There are many different philosophies and approaches toward currency management, and the hedging instruments mentioned here can be used in a variety of legitimate styles and methods. Currency management can be achieved through passive and active strategies, and can be implemented by the underlying international investment managers as well as by currency overlay "specialists."

---

[6]Sharpe and Alexander, *Investments* (4th Edition).

PASSIVE CURRENCY MANAGEMENT

Passive hedging involves the continuous conversion of foreign currencies back to the U.S. dollar, usually through the use of currency forward contracts. A currency forward contract is an agreement made today to exchange a predetermined amount of a foreign currency for the U.S. dollar at a specified date in the future. As existing currency forward contracts mature, new ones are entered into, and this process continues for as long as the underlying position in non-U.S. dollar securities exists. This continuous conversion process removes the portfolio's explicit exposure to foreign currencies; thus, the risk that remains is the risk inherent in the local securities market.[7]

Passive (or continuous) hedging requires frequent transactions in all currencies, however, leading to the possibility of high transactions costs. Depending on the hedging instruments used in a passive program, such trading activity might necessitate the maintenance of high cash balances to support the hedges. The maintenance of such cash balances entails an opportunity cost because such cash cannot be invested in other, more productive assets (e.g., stocks, bonds, etc.).[8]

ACTIVE CURRENCY MANAGEMENT

Active hedging could involve the use of futures, forwards, options, and actual currencies so as to manage exchange rate risk.

Active hedging strategies employed by the underlying securities portfolio manager offer the *possibility* of more favorable return patterns than a passive strategy. Mark Kritzman demonstrated that central banks, in their desire to stabilize currency values, effectively induce non-randomness into exchange rates, and that this situation can persist for prolonged periods.[9] As a result, an active approach toward currency management can be successful because of the tendency for active strategies to profit from trending markets. Due to the nonrandomness of exchange rates, return enhancements are possible with an active strategy versus a passive one. At the same time, an active approach can actually experience lower transactions costs because of the potential for smaller cash reserve requirements and lower turnover than a passive approach's continual

---

[7]Carol W. Proffer, "To Hedge or Not to Hedge (Part II)," *Managing Currency Risk* (Charlottesville: AIMR, 1989).

[8]Stephen L. Nesbitt, "Currency Hedging Rules for Plan Sponsors," Wilshire Associates Research Report, August 1990.

[9]Mark P. Kritzman, "Hedging Opportunities," *Managing Currency Risk* (Charlottesville: AIMR, 1989).

conversion process. The downside is that if the active strategy is unsuccessful, there may be more risk and the potential for less favorable outcomes than a passive approach.[10]

Although it is conceptually appealing to delegate active currency management duties to the investment managers of the underlying international securities portfolios, some of these portfolio managers are neither accustomed to nor comfortable with actively hedging currency risk and should not be delegated such responsibility. For example, international stock managers tend to be relatively less comfortable with actively managing currency risk than international bond managers for reasons that will be discussed later in this chapter

Just as there are different styles of active securities management, there are different styles of active currency management. Some of these active styles rely more on fundamental approaches (e.g., purchasing power parity relationships), while others are "technical" in that they rely more on the trending nature of currency markets.[11] Another classification scheme separates currency management styles into defensive versus aggressive camps. The defensive styles primarily (but not exclusively) provide downside protection against adverse currency movements, while the aggressive styles primarily (but not exclusively) seek to generate a positive rate of return through active currency management. Regardless of the merit of some of these aggressive currency management strategies, their primary focus on return enhancement is at odds with the pure concept of currency hedging as a form of insurance, and may be more appropriate for those seeking trading profits rather than downside protection or risk control.

IMPLEMENTATION METHODS

There are two major methods for implementing a currency hedging program: using existing international securities managers and using an overlay manager.

A plan sponsor could delegate responsibility for currency management to existing external investment managers that use currency hedging within their international portfolios. In some cases, such portfolio managers are ideally suited to implement such strategies because they have a unique, macro-level perspective of their specific portfolio, and can make currency decisions that best fit their philosophies. This is typically

---

[10]Stephen L. Nesbitt and Margaret M. Drew, "Should Currency Exposure Be Managed?," Wilshire Associates Research Report, May 1991.

[11]Kritzman, "Hedging Opportunities."

the case with international and global fixed-income managers, who have a tendency to integrate currency management into their investment processes due to the commonality of factors affecting both exchange rates and interest rates. On the other hand, many international and global stock managers are less comfortable with making active, strategic currency decisions as a part of their broader portfolio management duties, preferring to focus on what they do best — top-down country selection and/or bottom-up stock selection to add value versus a benchmark. Moreover, many of these international stock managers often invest in countries with currencies that cannot be hedged effectively or efficiently due to the lack of a well-developed forward market or prohibitively high costs. International bond managers, on the other hand, tend to focus on investment opportunities in the G-7 countries where currency hedging can be accomplished with relative ease.

Should the plan sponsor elect to delegate currency hedging authority to the underlying investment managers, careful consideration must be given to the use of currency hedged benchmarks. The use of a partial or fully hedged benchmark allows the plan sponsor to communicate their normal level of risk tolerance with regard to currency exposure. For example, a plan sponsor with a high degree of risk tolerance and little regard for currency movements might elect to use an unhedged benchmark, while a plan sponsor more concerned with the effects of currency movements might elect to use a partially hedged or fully hedged benchmark.

Another implementation method involves use of an overlay manager as a currency expert who is superimposed over some or all of the existing international portfolio managers. Rather than have each international manager hedge those currencies in their respective accounts, the overlay manager would hedge with knowledge of the plan's total international exposure. For this method to work, the plan sponsor must periodically inform the overlay manager of the plan's optimal normal hedge ratio, the chosen "normal" international portfolio, and the market value of the underlying portfolio.

Unlike traditional investment managers, currency overlay managers do not receive "allocations" equal to the size of their mandate, as only a small cash reserve (usually less than 5%) is typically necessary to institute a hedging program. For example, an overlay manager with responsibility for hedging a $500 million international portfolio at a 50% hedge ratio might receive actual cash from the plan sponsor equal to only $12.5 million (5% × 50% × $500 million).[12] The cash reserve would be used,

---

[12]Nesbitt and Drew, "Should Currency Exposure Be Managed?"

for example, as margin to support currency futures positions. If the currency hedging program used currency forwards, the cash reserve would not be necessary since forwards typically do not require the use of margin.

THE CURRENCY HEDGING DEBATE

Any serious research effort on the topic of currency management should begin with a literature review of relevant articles and publications addressing this matter. The practitioner or student conducting such a review is likely to be simultaneously intrigued and frustrated, however, as there is little, if any, consensus regarding currency management policies and practices. For every intelligent, respected professional who has a view on this matter, there is another equally respected, intelligent professional with an opposing point of view. A sampling of these different views follows.

1. *"Always Hedge."* Perold and Schulman initiated the recent currency hedging debate in 1988.[13] They suggested that a fully hedged currency position offered an opportunity for a "free lunch" because the hedged position reduced the volatility of international portfolios without sacrificing returns over the long run.

2. *"Never Hedge."* Rosenberg, on the other hand, disagreed with the "free lunch" concept, noting that a hedged position, at least in foreign bonds, reduced the diversification benefits of such securities, which, in turn, made such portfolios less efficient than hedged portfolios.[14] He further noted that the costs associated with currency hedging make it a very expensive method to achieve diversification.

3. *"Half Hedge."* A prominent institutional investment consulting firm, RogersCasey, stated that any evaluation of currency hedging must consider past experience, and that such experience is highly time-period dependent.[15] The research report noted that

---

[13]Andre F. Perold and Evan C. Schulman, "The Free Lunch in Currency Hedging: Implications for Investment Policy and Performance Standards," *Financial Analysts Journal* (May/June 1988).

[14]Michael Rosenberg, "Hedging a Non-Dollar Fixed-Income Portfolio," *Managing Currency Risk* (Charlottesville: AIMR, 1989).

[15]"To Hedge or Not to Hedge? A Policy Discussion," Rogers, Casey & Associates Brief, October 1993.

the U.S. dollar rose in value between 1980 and 1985, and had fallen in value (generally) through 1993. Thus, the report concluded that neither a 0% hedged policy nor a 100% hedged policy is likely to be optimal, with the appropriate size of the currency hedge somewhere in between these two extremes, perhaps at a 50% hedge level from a strategic policy standpoint.

4. *"It Depends."* Proffer took a practical view on this subject, in which she argued that hedging is probably desirable, but that plan sponsors must weigh the benefits of hedging against the costs.[16] She also noted that the specific needs of the plan sponsor must also be evaluated before determining whether or not to hedge currencies.

SUGGESTED FRAMEWORK FOR DECISION-MAKING

With so much conflicting information on the topic of currency hedging, the plan sponsor is placed in an uncomfortable position when deciding which route to take. The factors supporting the argument for an actively managed currency program were presented earlier in this chapter. If a plan sponsor leans toward an active strategy, should it be accomplished via an overlay manager or by the managers of the underlying securities portfolios? Jorion has suggested that an overlay approach can add value if the actual investment managers of the underlying stock or bond portfolios lack currency expertise, but that plan sponsors would still be better off identifying and hiring a single adviser who can jointly manage both a securities portfolio and currencies.[17]

In a perfect world, the managers of the underlying international stock and bond portfolios would undertake currency management responsibility. The problem, however, is that not all international investment managers have the ability or capacity to manage currency risk in a meaningful manner. The tendency for some (but not all) international stock managers to ignore currency risk is a major reason why the use of a currency overlay manager is warranted under such circumstances. The other alternative would be for the plan sponsor to hire or retain only those international stock managers with the internal capability to manage currency risk in a meaningful manner. Clearly, there are a few large,

---

[16]Carol W. Proffer, "To Hedge or Not to Hedge (Part II)," *Managing Currency Risk* (Charlottesville: AIMR, 1989).

[17]Philippe Jorion, "Mean/Variance Analysis of Currency Overlays," *Financial Analysts Journal* (May/June 1994).

global firms with the necessary resources to handle such an assignment at this time. The solution that works best for each U.S. pension plan will ultimately depend on (1) the plan sponsor's level of comfort (or lack thereof) in delegating currency management responsibilities to investment managers of underlying international stock and bond portfolios, and (2) the costs associated with various hedging strategies. Should the plan sponsor delegate currency management responsibility to the underlying international investment managers, currency hedging costs could be as high as 25 basis points annually. If, however, a separate currency overlay manager is hired to handle this role, then the resulting management fees of approximately 30 basis points could bring the total annual costs to as high as 55 basis points.[18]

Once this decision is made, the next important decision regards the quantity of international investments that should be covered by a currency hedging program. In an article that appeared in the Fall 1995 issue of the *Journal of Portfolio Management*, the author proposed that a mean-variance analysis on an entire portfolio should be conducted as a starting point to determine the appropriate normal size of a strategic currency hedge. The analysis would take into account the expectational inputs — expected returns, standard deviations, and correlations — of all asset classes *and currency exposures* within the investment program, as well as the expected costs associated with currency hedging.[19]

The expectational inputs used in the optimization analysis can be derived from historical records, and should be modified to reflect current market valuations. Although currency values versus the U.S. dollar do change and, hence, have correlations, returns, and standard deviations of return, the long-run *expected* return on a pure currency exposure alone is proposed to be zero. The costs associated with currency hedging are often overlooked but are vitally important; as was noted, these costs can be as high as 55 basis points annually in the most extreme circumstances. Many optimizers allow for costs to be assigned to various asset classes; in the absence of this ability, the expected return for currencies can be entered as a negative number to reflect the long run assertion that currencies have an inherent expected return of 0% in the long run but that hedging them does entail costs.

The optimization procedure results in the generation of a series of efficient portfolios with varying degrees of currency exposures. The

---

[18]The author is grateful to Reza Vishkai, a consultant at RogersCasey, Darien, CT, for furnishing this information.

[19]Joseph A. Braccia, "An Analysis of Currency Overlays for U.S. Pension Plans," *Journal of Portfolio Management* (Fall 1995).

plan sponsor would then select a portfolio along the efficient frontier that best reflects their risk tolerance and return requirements, just as they normally would in any other optimization procedure. If the optimization process produces one or more sample efficient portfolios with a normal currency hedge position greater than 0%, then a strategic currency hedge should have a role for the plan sponsor. If the optimization process produces a series of portfolios with a normal currency hedge position at or close to 0%, then a strategic currency hedge would be superfluous in term of risk reduction.

The author's previously cited optimization analysis revealed that in a hypothetical an unrealistic no-cost environment, significant use of currency hedging was preferred. Yet, when costs were factored in to the equation, the optimizer's strong preference for currency hedging was altered. An assumption that the costs associated with currency hedging totaled 55 basis points produced a series of efficient portfolios with little or no amount of strategic currency hedging. Because of the presence of transactions costs and other fees, the optimizer found more efficient methods of constructing optimal portfolios. To put it another way, the hypothetical and extreme 55 basis point cost of "insurance" (or risk reduction) through currency hedging made it more feasible to bear currency risk by avoiding a strategic currency hedge.[20]

The optimization analysis intentionally used two extreme cost assumptions (a zero-cost assumption and a 55 basis point cost assumption) merely to illustrate the elasticity of demand for currency hedging. The truth is that the actual costs associated with currency hedging are almost certainly somewhere between these two extremes. A series of optimization analyses using a rising scale of hedging costs between zero and 55 basis points should confirm that there is an inverse relationship between the demand for the product (i.e., currency hedging) and the product's total cost.

A CAVEAT ABOUT THE FUTURE

We know that the future will be different from the past — but how will it differ? With regard to currency management, it is important to remember that historical relationships among currencies might not hold in the future. For example, as more countries implement the capitalist model on a broader scale, new investment opportunities and risks will emerge - including risks associated with currency exposure. The potential for a single currency in Europe will alter, but not eliminate, currency risks

---

[20]Braccia, "An Analysis of Currency Overlays for U.S. Pension Plans."

associated with investments in Germany, the United Kingdom, etc. Finally, currencies of some countries are currently pegged to the U.S. dollar, but such practices should not be viewed as being permanent. One need only consider the turmoil that engulfed Asian currency markets beginning in mid-1997 to realize that currency pegging should be viewed as a temporary measure.

The point is that an optimization analysis, for example, is only as good as the data entered into the optimizer itself; the old computer programmer's lament, "garbage in, garbage out," is appropriate to keep in mind here. An optimizer is a powerful tool that can reduce the subjective tendency to select an easy, "feel good" solution to a complex problem, but the user must simultaneously recognize an optimizer's limitations, particularly in an era of rapid financial innovation and economic change. The key, therefore, is for plan sponsors to identify the most rational instances of how the future might be different from the past, and to incorporate these factors into their investment decision-making processes. This should be done regardless of whether an optimization analysis or some other procedure is used to help address the thorny issue of currency management.

SUMMARY

The decision to hedge or not to hedge currencies will depend upon the plan sponsor's profile, and would consider factors such as the size of the international allocation, the costs associated with hedging, and the ability to identify and hire talented managers to implement such strategies. An optimization analysis that takes into account the costs of hedging is an excellent objective exercise to help assess the potential role of a strategic currency management program.

Should a plan sponsor determine that a strategic currency hedge makes sense, an actively managed approach is recommended because of cost and return considerations. Of the active strategies, the most relevant are those that are defensive or risk-controlled in nature rather than those that principally seek to generate positive total returns. Ideally, currency hedging programs should be implemented by the underlying international investment managers, but this might not be feasible given the nature in which some investment managers operate. Under these circumstances, the best solution is to consider hiring a currency overlay manager as a specialist to handle all or most aspects of a strategic currency management program.

A plan sponsor contemplating the initiation of a strategic currency hedging program should be adequately prepared for a lengthy and often challenging research process. There are few (if any) obvious answers, and each apparent "solution" seemingly raises more issues that must be addressed. Moreover, the administrative burden associated with implementing and monitoring a currency hedging program can be quite intense. In summary, while currency management is a challenging and perplexing subject, it is an area that must be addressed by plan sponsors in an era of global investing, economic change, and heightened risk awareness.

John A. de Luna is a principal with State Street Global Advisors, effective August 1998.

Prior to joining SSgA, deLuna spent eight years as vice president of Scudder Kemper Investments, Inc. As director of marketing for the $13 billion Reserve Asset Management Group, he was responsible for business development.

Earlier in his professional career, de Luna established a trust and investment management presence on the West Coast for Irving Trust and the Bank of New York. He also spent seven years with Crocker Bank, responsible for interest rate hedging product sales. At Crocker, de Luna was responsible for foreign central bank relationships in the capital markets group and served in the international division as assistant regional manager to the Andean Pact countries in Latin America.

De Luna received his bachelor of science degree in psychology in 1976 from Santa Clara University and a juris doctor from the Santa Clara University School of Law in 1979. He is currently on the board of directors of the Mexican-American Bar Foundation and is a mentor to the Toigo Foundation Fellows Program.

Chapter 8

Managing Short-Term Investment Funds

John A. de Luna
Principal
State Street Global Advisors

When looking at portfolio management strategy, the cash portion is often written off as nothing more than an unavoidable but essential necessity. It frequently receives little or no attention from plan sponsors. Many times, the cash portion is maintained simply to take advantage of market opportunities and/or to hedge against sudden market swings. We believe that this traditional view and treatment of cash management is often skewed by some key inaccurate assumptions. Among these are the assumptions that true cash is only a small portion of an overall portfolio and that the cash portion carries little or no risk.

In this chapter, we will examine more closely these traditional approaches to cash. We will discuss an area of "forgotten cash" easily overlooked by plan sponsors, as well some ways in which cash investing can become perilous. We will also examine and challenge the widely held idea that short-term investment funds are the best and least expensive repository for cash; instead, we will propose separate account management as a wiser and less costly alternative.

HIGH-END/LOW END CASH POSITIONS
To begin, it is helpful to understand how much of a typical portfolio may be in cash. It is common for the average cash positions of equity and fixed-income managers to range from a low of 3% to a high of 12% of the total portfolio. Whether the variance is due to investment style, market conditions (or the perception of these conditions), or the need for liquidity to meet operating liabilities, these percentages — which at first glance may seem relatively inconsequential — can add up to very substantial assets. A real-life example may make this clearer. Scudder, Kemper Investments, Inc. manages a short-term portfolio for a large public fund in Southern California. The fund's total portfolio is approximately $20 billion; thus a cash position of 3% to 12% translates into an amount of $600 million in cash on the low end and $2.4 billion on the high end. These are

significant dollar amounts that should compel an investor with a portfolio even one-tenth this size to pay closer attention to its management.

Yet these kinds of numbers are often only the tip of the iceberg. In many cases, the largest amount of cash, frequently overlooked or misunderstood by plan sponsors, is the area of securities lending. Simply put, this is the process by which a securities lender (in most cases the custody bank) lends out, on a short-term basis, portions of the portfolio holdings, in exchange for cash collateral. The lender pays an interest rate on the cash and reinvests it, with the objective of earning more on reinvestment of the cash than it pays to the borrower of the security.

Because of the short-term focus of this strategy, many of these investments will be in the same sort of vehicles as in the recognized pure cash portion of the portfolio. The securities lending portion of a portfolio varies, but typically averages between 30% and 80%. While not all collateral is in cash, a significant portion is. In the case of the public fund we previously discussed, for example, if we assume conservatively that 50% of the portfolio is being lent at any given time and that 60% of this collateral is in cash, $6 billion of this plan's assets are actually in cash — in addition to the aforementioned, recognized $600 million to $2.4 billion. The area of securities lending has complexities and ramifications that cannot be discussed at length here. We mention it only to emphasize that it serves greatly (and covertly) to increase the cash balance of a portfolio.

THE RISK FACTOR

Another often inaccurate assumption about cash is that it carries little or no risk. Investors assume that since these assets are put into commonly used "safe" short-term instruments such as U.S. Treasuries, certificates of deposit, time deposits, commercial paper, and/or bankers acceptances, this portion of the portfolio therefore does not need to be vigilantly watched. While technically this may be correct, nearly every major money-management scandal that has occurred since the beginning of this decade has involved short-term investments. Often this occurs not because there is problem with the instruments themselves but because there is a problem with those charged with their management. More specifically, problems with these investments usually involve a manager (internal or external) undertaking a level of risk that differed from what participants or shareholders understood or were unwilling to accept.

Frank Fabozzi calls this "risk risk,"[1] the consequence of not

---

[1]Frank J. Fabozzi, "The Fundamentals of Fixed Income Securities," Chapter 10 in Frank J. Fabozzi (ed.) *Securities Lending and Repurchase Agreements*, Frank J. Fabozzi Associates (New Hope, Penn.: 1997), 127.

understanding the risks accepted by a manager. The factors behind these differences in accepted risk range from poor communication to ignorance to greed, from situations where managers made errors in judgment to those in which stated guidelines were blatantly violated. In this way an apparently riskless asset class can be laden with danger.

The above factor was clearly illustrated in the course of events with the Orange County Investment Pool in 1994. This short-term fund, designed to hold liquid assets for municipalities within the county, was administered by the county treasurer. Lured by high yields, he gradually converted these low-risk investments into a highly speculative account. The reporting was apparently vague and the treasurer never clearly revealed his holdings. Although many people, including the Orange County Board of Supervisors, should have been suspicious about how this fund was able to earn such high yields if it was truly following its investment guidelines, no one seemed to question its management. When interest rates went against the positions in the pool, the portfolio was deeply under water. Orange County was forced into bankruptcy to avoid the liability claims. The Orange County example illustrates how a fund intended for liquidity and safety can end up destroying the objective of an entire portfolio.

USE AND MISUSE OF CREDIT-QUALITY RATINGS

Additional problems can also arise from the belief that, regardless of their management, short-term investment vehicles are generic and follow a uniform standard. A good illustration of this kind of misunderstanding can be found in the use of credit quality ratings developed by Moody's, Standard & Poor's, and others. For example, when the guidelines for a given portfolio allow a rating described as "A1/P1" or similar rating by a "nationally recognized rating agency," there might be some confusion as to what this actually means and how it can be interpreted by a manager. Does this mean that instruments rated A1 or P1 are allowed, or that only those rated both A1 and P1 are allowed, or that neither an A1 or P1 is necessary if there is a similarly high rating from a nationally recognized rating agency? What qualifies as a "nationally recognized" rating agency? And so on. All of this underscores the need for a plan sponsor to choose its managers carefully, communicate with them clearly, know its investments well, and make well informed, consistently updated assessments on whether these instruments are meeting the needs of the plan.

SEPARATELY MANAGED ACCOUNTS

Not understanding the complexities involved in cash investments, many plan sponsors end up using short-term investment funds (STIFs) for their cash instead of using separately managed accounts — despite significant advantages to managed accounts and hidden dangers in the use of STIFs. In a STIF, for example, the investment strategies are designed for all the shareholders, and the interest of all shareholders is equal. The investor with $1 billion receives the same attention as the one with $5 million. A plan sponsor cannot restrict or modify the guidelines of the STIF. Some STIFs, for example, allow A2/P2 or "splits" such as A1/P2 (or A2/P1) rated paper. Also, since STIFs are relatively small revenue generators for a custodian, they tend to be managed by junior, less experienced investment staff — thus potentially increasing the risks previously described.

By contrast, a private and separately managed account is structured to specific and individualized guidelines. The attention is personalized and customized, and plan sponsors have total access to the people managing the portfolio. In general, STIFs exist for the benefit of the custodial bank, for which a STIF is a low-cost and convenient way to pool and manage cash for smaller investors. A separately managed account, on the other hand, exists for the benefit of the investor (the plan sponsor) itself. As an added bonus, separately managed accounts can actually be significantly less expensive than a STIF, particularly for a large investor. On average, STIF fees are between 12 and 20 basis points regardless of account balance; on many separately managed accounts, fees are lower (and negotiable).

In thinking about a separately managed cash account, the fundamental and essential considerations are safety of principal and maintenance of liquidity. To assure safety of principal, quality ratings for the investments in this type of portfolio should be clearly specified, regularly reviewed, and should reflect a plan sponsor's overall tolerance for risk. Also, careful thought and consideration should be given to the match between sector selection and portfolio manager to ensure that the chosen manager has sufficient experience and capability in a particular area or sector.

For example, durations of CMOs and mortgage- and asset-backed securities tend to lengthen during periods of rising interest rates. These extending durations may place them in violation of maturity guidelines for a given portfolio. If a plan sponsor chooses to invest in these sectors, it is essential that he has a manager who thoroughly understands how these investments operate and can manage them skillfully and actively.

Maturity guidelines for cash portfolios should be somewhat flexible but clearly in line with the preservation of capital. The portfolio should be managed to a maturity benchmark with a low probability for loss. Exhibit 1 reviews 68 quarterly periods for various indices from 1981 to the fourth quarter of 1997. The indices with no quarterly loss history — the three-month T-bill index, six-month T-bill index, and one-year bill Index — can be prime candidates for consideration as benchmarks since they meet the chief consideration of safety of principal.

Exhibit 1: Negative Quarters As a Percent of Total Period; Q1 1981 - Q4 1997 (68 Quarters)

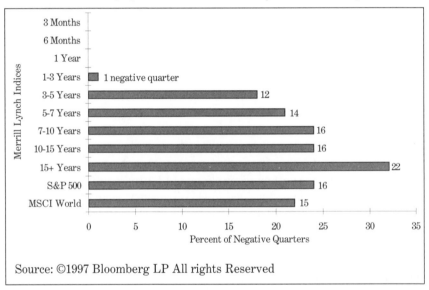

Source: ©1997 Bloomberg LP All rights Reserved

Exhibit 2 confirms that these indices experience the lowest level of volatility. Portfolio maturities beyond these benchmarks can be utilized if they are in line with the plan sponsor's risk tolerance. In addition, plan sponsors should specify a maximum maturity to ensure that the entire portfolio is within safe guidelines. In general the average maturity bands around the benchmark generally should not exceed +/-25%.

To provide for the other paramount objective, liquidity, the portfolio can be structured in a number of different ways. One of these might include establishing a guideline restriction which requires that a certain percentage of the portfolio be maintained with a maturity level of less

Exhibit 2: Merrill Lynch Government and Equity Indices Volatility of Returns - Q1 1981-Q4 1997

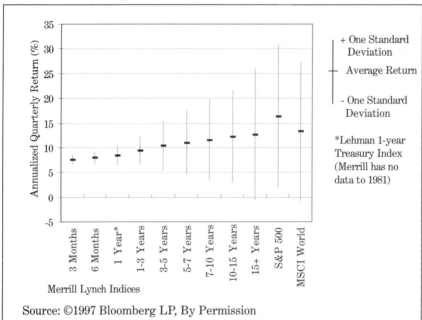

Source: ©1997 Bloomberg LP, By Permission

than three months. Another example would be to require that at least 25% of the portfolio be maintained in U.S. Treasury securities.

Yield enhancement in a cash portfolio is icing on the cake and should be pursued as a goal only after preservation of principal and liquidity have been ensured. Indeed, the riskiest situations for cash portfolios arise when the priorities become reversed and yield enhancement becomes primary. Often, a skilled manager can effectively enhance yield by extending maturities and diversifying sectors, as discussed earlier. One typical way of enhancing yields — lowering the credit quality — should be strictly avoided, no matter how tempting the possible returns. The lowering of tolerable ratings is often a slippery slope which directly contradicts the primary goal of preservation of capital.

CONCLUSION
It is our hope that this chapter has dispelled some of the myths surrounding cash assets and has illuminated topics in short-term portfolio management which might not always receive adequate attention and focus. By paying more attention to the opportunities and the hazards

involved in short-term asset management, these portfolios can be more secure, more cost-effective, and, quite possibly, more profitable.

John R. Caswell, CFA, is a senior portfolio manager and principal of Galliard Capital Management, based in Minneapolis, involved in policy and strategy formulation for the firm's stable-value and fixed-income portfolios. Caswell has more than two decades of experience in the investment management industry.

Prior to co-founding Galliard, he served as chief investment officer for Norwest Investment Management.

Caswell holds a bachelor of arts degree and a master's degree in business administration from the University of Iowa.

Karl Tourville is a senior portfolio manager and principal of Galliard Capital Management. In this capacity, he is involved in asset selection and strategy formulation for the firm's stable-value and fixed-income portfolios.

Prior to co-founding Galliard, Tourville was vice president and manager of taxable fixed-income portfolios for Norwest Investment Management, where he oversaw approxmately $3 billion in assets.

Tourville has over nine years of investment management experience. He is an adjunct professor of finance at the University of St. Thomas Graduate School of Business, St. Paul, and is a past board member of the Stable Value Association.

Tourville holds a bachelor of arts degree and a master's degree in business administration from the University of St. Thomas.

Chapter 9

The Case for Stable-Value Pension Investments

John R. Caswell, CFA
Principal
Galliard Capital Management

Karl P. Tourville
Principal
Galliard Capital Management

The rapid formation and widespread use of defined-contribution pension plans in the United States over the last 15-20 years has significantly impacted the U.S. financial markets. During this period, assets in defined-contribution (DC) plans grew from about $90 billion to $2.3 trillion in 1997. While the corporate sector, through the popular 401(k) plan, has led the way in this explosive growth trend with over $1.7 trillion of total DC assets, most states and numerous municipalities have also established deferred-compensation (457) plans for employees that operate similarly to their corporate cousin, the 401(k).

Public plans have accumulated over $100 billion in assets to date, now representing one of the fastest-growing segments of the DC market. The key feature of all of these plans that has profoundly impacted investment management trends has been the shift in responsibility for investment decision-making from plan sponsors to individual plan participants. For conservative participants whose primary investment objective is preservation of capital, stable-value investments have been widely used in both the corporate and public plan sectors due their attractive yields, stability, and safety.

A stable-value investment is an instrument in which contractual terms provide for a guaranteed return of principal at specified rate of interest. Examples of stable-value assets include fixed annuities and traditional guaranteed investment contracts (GICS), bank investment contracts (BICs), and GIC alternatives such as separate-account GICs and synthetic GICs. Stable-value pooled funds, which are professionally managed collective trusts investing in these assets, are also utilized. Growth

in stable-value assets has paralleled that of the overall defined-contribution market, rising to over $250 billion today from $29 billion in 1984.

A key feature of a stable-value asset is its treatment from an
accounting standpoint. According to Generally Accepted Accounting
Principles (GAAP), stable-value instruments can be held at contract
value, provided that established criteria are met. Contract value is the
acquisition cost of the contract plus accrued interest, adjusted to reflect
any additional deposits or withdrawals. This is also referred to as book
value. Book-value accounting eliminates the market-value fluctuations
experienced by other asset classes and contributes to the high, risk-
adjusted returns of stable-value instruments.

Initially, traditional GICs were the dominant stable-value instrument. This was true of the corporate market initially and remains the
case for a majority of the public fund plans. The perceived risk in these
products was minimal and they faced little, if any, competition until the
insolvency of several major GIC issuers. While these defaults proved to
be a great challenge to an industry unaccustomed to such difficulties,
they also proved to be the catalyst for tremendous change resulting in
the development of a new generation of products, popularly known as
synthetic GICs. Investors, and ultimately plan participants, now benefit
from a broader variety of products, providers, and strategies.

This chapter will review the various instruments utilized in
today's stable value portfolios with an emphasis on GIC alternatives, the
most rapidly growing segment of the market. Also discussed are contract
terms and portfolio management considerations along with some
thoughts on the future direction of the stable-value asset class.

STABLE-VALUE PRODUCTS

Investment Contracts(GICs and BICs)

Traditional guaranteed investment contracts (also called guaranteed
insurance, interest, or income contracts) were the foundation of today's
stable-value industry. A GIC is issued by an insurance company, utilizing
a group annuity contract format. As insurance contracts, the obligation is
backed by the general account of the issuer. In an effort to diversify its
depositor base and obtain funding at attractive rates, the banking industry began issuing competing bank investment contracts (BICs) in 1987.
While providing stable-value portfolios with industry diversification,
BICs achieved only modest market share as a limited number of issuers
constrained supply.

While different in legal structure and regulatory purview, GICs and BICs are functionally similar in that the issuer of the contract receives a deposit of funds from a qualified investor and, in return, guarantees a specified rate of interest for a predetermined period of time. Interest is accrued on either a simple interest or a fully compounded basis and paid either annually or at the end of the contract term. The contracts include a variety of terms (discussed later), the most important of which is a guarantee that payments will be made at the contract's book value for qualified participant withdrawals. This feature allows these contracts to be valued at their book value rather than at some calculated market value equivalent.

While traditional GICs still play an important role in most stable-value portfolios, diversification considerations relative to life insurance industry exposure have led to their diminishing use vis-à-vis GIC alternatives. Although some portfolios have significant investments in traditional GICs, more often these products are evaluated versus other investment alternatives and purchased on the basis of their relative value — similar to corporate bonds in a marketable bond portfolio.

GIC Alternatives

Designed to preserve the benefits of traditional GICs while providing added portfolio diversification and investor control, GIC alternatives now account for a significant and increasing amount of the stable-value marketplace. The two primary forms of alternatives are separate-account GICs offered through life insurance companies; and synthetic contracts issued by insurance companies, banks, and other financial institutions.

Separate-Account GICs

Separate-account GICs are the closest cousins to traditional GICs in that they are contractually issued as a group annuity policy with terms negotiated between the parties. However, unlike a GIC — which is backed by the general assets of the issuer — in a separate account, the insurance company segregates the assets on its balance sheet for the exclusive benefit of the contract holder. Legal ownership remains with the insurance company, but the contract holder's beneficial interest in the securities has been clearly established in most states. Therefore, in the event of an insolvency, the assets are not subject to claims of general policy holders.

The separate-account assets may be managed by the insurance company or, in some cases, by an outside money manager selected by the contract holder with the approval of the insurance company. An initial crediting rate of interest is established which reflects the yield of the underlying securities as well as the insurance company's underwriting, administration, and investment management fees.

The contract may have a specific maturity date or the assets may be managed to a constant duration, in which case the contract has no specified maturity date (referred to as "evergreen"). Additional flexibility is provided to the contract holder within this structure to establish individual investment guidelines for maturity, credit quality, and diversification. A variety of terms and conditions may be included in the contract, but the key feature is the provision for payments to plan participants at book value for qualified withdrawals.

Synthetic GICs

Synthetic GICs provide the features of a separate-account GIC with the additional advantage that the contract holder retains actual ownership and custody of the assets underlying the contract. In a typical synthetic structure, the investor purchases a fixed-income security (or portfolio of securities) and enters into a contract with a third-party guarantor. This third party is typically a bank or an insurance company, which agrees to accommodate benefit payments and other qualified participant withdrawals at the contract's book value. The contract is typically referred to as a wrapper agreement, and the issuer is called a wrap provider.

The investor retains ownership of the underlying pool of securities and receives an interest crediting rate equal to the annualized effective yield of the securities with an adjustment for fees and other factors. Additionally, the contract guarantees the investor a minimum rate of interest, usually 0%, to protect against a loss of principal. In exchange for these considerations, the wrap provider receives a fee that varies according to the risk assumed.

A synthetic GIC arrangement may involve as many as four parties, including an investor, a wrap provider, an outside money manager, and a trustee/custodian. One financial institution may provide all services for an investor (bundled product) or the service providers may be different entities (unbundled product). Regardless of the parties involved, the structural mechanics are similar. The terms of the wrap agreement transform a portfolio of marketable securities, whose values fluctuate, into a synthetic GIC.

Buy-and-Hold Synthetics

In a buy-and-hold synthetic structure, the investor purchases a single security which is usually held to its final maturity. The contract's crediting rate generally remains fixed, although rate resets may occur if expected or actual cash flows change. In these respects, buy-and-hold synthetics closely resemble traditional GICs. To date, asset-backed and mortgage-backed securities have been used heavily in buy-and-hold structures due to their high credit quality and relatively attractive yields. The buy-and-hold synthetic can also be structured with an interest rate swap embedded within a wrap agreement. With this version of the product, a floating-rate security is purchased and the floating interest rate is exchanged for a fixed rate. A wide array of features have been used in these arrangements, although use of callable, extendible, or amortizable (based on the performance of an index) structures have been most common.

Actively Managed Synthetics

The rationale behind the utilization of managed synthetics is the belief that active investment management enhances investment returns and leads to higher contract crediting rates. Added benefits include broader diversification and the ability to buy and sell securities or adjust the portfolio's duration, which enhances flexibility. Portfolios are constructed using the full range of fixed-income securities including U.S. Treasuries and agencies, mortgage-backed and asset-backed securities, and corporate bonds.

More complex instruments, such as interest rate swaps, futures, and options are also utilized, although to a lesser degree. The interest earned by investors over time equals the total return on the underlying portfolio of securities, less wrap and investment management fees. With managed synthetics, the volatility of annual returns is greatly reduced because of book value accounting. Exhibit 1 illustrates the smoothing effects of a wrap contract on a portfolio of marketable securities. Quarterly returns from the Lehman Brothers Intermediate Government/Corporate Bond Index are charted over a recent 10-year period. Overlaid on this exhibit are the returns that would have resulted in each period had the index had been wrapped, net of annual wrap fees of 0.15%. As can be seen, the wrapped portfolio's quarterly returns are considerably more stable.

Managed synthetics are available in two forms, immunized and constant duration (evergreen). An immunized contract has a fixed maturity and, hence, the duration of the underlying portfolio is lowered over time to meet the maturity date. Evergreen contracts are managed within established duration bands and a specific maturity date is not usually established. To date, evergreen contracts have been the most commonly used managed synthetic.

Exhibit 1: Quarterly Return Comparisons
January 1987-December 1996

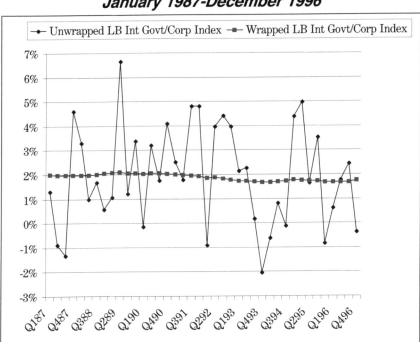

Alpha Synthetics

A newer hybrid referred to as the alpha synthetic combines the characteristics of the buy-and-hold and managed structures. In the alpha structure, an interest rate swap is embedded in a wrap contract. The investor agrees to pay the total return of an established benchmark for a specified period of time in exchange for a fixed rate of return known as the base rate. The base rate paid is a function of current Treasury yields and interest rate swap spreads relative to the index selected. The portfolio is then actively managed to outperform the selected index and any positive performance margin, referred to as portfolio alpha, is earned by the investor.

The initial crediting rate usually equals the base rate less wrap and investment management fees. Sometimes an estimate of the expected outperformance of the manager is added to the base rate to establish the initial crediting rate. The crediting rate is then reset periodically, often annually, to reflect the actual performance of the portfolio.

Stable-Value Pooled Funds

Individual stable-value portfolios may typically invest in most, if not all, of the products described in this chapter. However, many employee benefit plans have opted to utilize a professionally managed stable-value collective fund rather than attempt to manage their own portfolio. This is especially true in small to midsize plans, where it is increasingly difficult to attain appropriate portfolio diversification without incurring significant transaction costs. In addition, many larger plans utilize a pooled fund vehicle as a buffer within their portfolio to provide immediate liquidity for qualified withdrawals. Such a liquidity fund or buffer is often a contractual requirement stipulated by the issuer to minimize the likelihood of tapping its contracts for book-value payments. For that reason, investing in a stable-value collective fund can serve to enhance a portfolio's overall yield given that, over time, it outperforms shorter-term investments such as money market funds.

Stable-value pooled funds operate similar to mutual funds except that they are exempt from registration as securities with the Securities and Exchange Commission. The funds are collective trusts offered through banks and trust companies to fiduciary clients and can accept only qualified employee benefit plans as investors — including any plan qualified under section 401(a) of the Internal Revenue Service Code and deferred-compensation plans described in section 457 of the Code. The funds are typically valued daily in the same way as mutual funds and, therefore, offer substantial flexibility to a plan sponsor for investing participant contributions and paying out plan benefits. Pooled funds invest in the full range of stable-value products, offering to a plan ongoing professional management, broad diversification, high credit quality, and competitive returns.

THE EVOLUTION OF STABLE VALUE

Having defined the various stable-value products available today, a review of the market from an historical perspective may provide some insight into both the current use of these products within the context of portfolio management and where stable value may evolve in the future.

The Beginnings

Following enactment of the Employee Retirement Income and Security Act of 1974 (ERISA), the concept began to emerge of plan participants directing their own investments in defined-contribution plans. A significant result of this legislation was the increased utilization of guaranteed annuity contracts (GACs), which would hold a dominant position within these plans for years to come. Offered by the life insurance industry, which has been in the forefront of pension development and management in the United States, the GAC (also referred to as an immediate participation guarantee contract) was a nonmaturing contract featuring a fixed rate of interest that was convertible to an individual annuity upon retirement. This option was popular until the substantial rise in interest rates in the late 1970s and early 1980s, when the comparatively low rates of interest of the GAC created dissatisfaction among participants versus the double-digit, short-term market rates available at the time. These events prompted the creation of the guaranteed investment contract (GIC) of today, which retained the fixed-rate feature while offering relatively short, set maturity dates to allow for more rapid reinvestment and competitive returns.

Concurrent with these events, there were significant overhauls in the U.S. tax code, ultimately providing for tax-deferred contributions by participants to qualified employee benefit plans — including the 401(k) plan. These modifications prompted explosive growth in defined contribution plan formation, rising employee participation, and placed the investment decision-making responsibility in the hands of the individual plan participant. GICs were easy to understand. The fixed-rate, fixed-maturity structure was quite similar to bank certificates of deposit (CDs), so they were a likely beneficiary of the changes and grew rapidly. This growth attracted competition and, in 1987, a limited number of banks began issuing BICs to compete with GICs.

During this period, many plan sponsors managed their GIC options internally and purchased GIC and BIC contracts directly from the issuers or through consultants or GIC brokers. Some plans utilized a single insurance company's GIC, offering either a class year structure (participants received a new rate each year on their contributions) or a blended rate, which changed each year. In an effort to provide a diversified GIC option to smaller plans or to larger plans in their startup phase, many banks began offering GIC pooled funds in the mid-1980s. These funds featured independent professional management, credit oversight, diversification, and a mutual-fund-type structure and liquidity (subject to certain restrictions).

The Rise of Alternatives (Synthetics)

Traditional GICs were thought to be relatively safe, offering a guarantee of principal and interest to the participant. This perception began to change in the wake of the savings & loan crisis of the late 1980s, which was accompanied by credit concerns about banks and insurance companies, as well. It culminated with the default and seizure of Executive Life by the California state insurance commissioner in 1991.

In response to the growing credit and diversification concerns of GIC investors, Bankers Trust began offering the first synthetic GIC alternative in 1990, called BASIC — benefits accessible securities investment contract — which provided a book-value guarantee (wrapper) on an individual marketable fixed-income security. Bankers Trust followed in 1991 with the managed BASIC, which wrapped a portfolio of securities.

As synthetics gradually filtered into the marketplace, Bankers Trust was one of a limited number of active issuers. Purchasers of these early products tended to be more sophisticated investors, such as plan sponsors that managed their pension plans internally or professional stable-value managers. Following the highly publicized defaults of Mutual Benefit Life (1992) and Confederation Life (1994), however, synthetic GICs became widely used to enhance portfolio diversification and to reduce credit risk.

A time line of key market developments appears in Exhibit 2. The insurance industry quickly followed Bankers Trust's lead. It responded with a wrap contract of its own as well as increased efforts to market separate account GICs that offer features similar to wrapper agreements, although asset ownership and custody remained with the insurance company. Pooled funds also grew in popularity as plan sponsors sought to hire outside fiduciaries to manage their portfolios following issuer defaults. The larger, well diversified pooled funds were found to be an attractive alternative to in-house management.

Exhibit 2: Evolution of Stable Value

GICs Evolve	BICs	Insurance Company Concerns	Bankers Trust Introduces BASIC	Exec Life	Mutual Benefit Life			Increasing Number of New Issuers Entering Market — Confederation Life			
1970/80s	1987	1989	1990	1991	1992	1993	1994	1995	1996	1997

15 Pooled Funds	GIC Alternatives	28 Pooled Funds
$3.7 Billion in Assets	Become Increasingly Popular	$28 Billion in Assets

Source: Hueler Analytics, by permission.

The Stable-Value Market Today

Because of its unique position in the defined contribution market, the stable-value market has evolved from the old GIC mantle to an entire industry with its own association. Many stable-value professionals are now advancing the argument that stable value is an asset class separate to itself, given its unique risk/return characteristics. Indeed, many plan sponsors and plan participants must agree, as stable-value assets, by some estimates, now exceed $250 billion. According to a recent IOMA survey of 119 large plan sponsors, stable-value assets represented over 75% of total fixed-income assets held in those plans.[1]

While traditional GICs are still the largest segment within the stable-value market, their dominance in the future is not assured. According to data released by the Life Insurance Marketing and Research Association (LIMRA) and the Stable Value Association, annual sales of synthetic GICs have increased an average of 30% each year since 1991, with total purchases during 1995 exceeding $15 billion.

During this same period, sales of traditional GICs declined an average of 8%, with $22 billion in sales during 1995. The migration toward synthetics has been especially prevalent among professional stable-value managers. According to Hueler Analytics, synthetic GICs accounted for 58.7% of all new purchases made by stable-value pooled funds in 1995. A breakdown of stable-value assets by product type is provided in Exhibit 3.

Exhibit 3: Product Market Share as of Dec. 31, 1996

	Total Assets $ Billion
Guaranteed investment contracts	142
Separate account contracts	31
Synthetic GICs	62
Other	15
Total	$250

Source: John Hancock, Life Insurance Marketing and Research Association (LIMRA) and the Stable Value Investment Association, by permission.

Enticed by rising demand and relatively attractive fees, numerous wrap providers have now entered the market. Banks, including the domestic branches of foreign institutions, now dominate with an estimated 68% share of total wrapped assets. Insurance companies, despite some restrictions that have limited their ability to provide synthetics, have captured 32% of the market. A list of active wrap providers appears in Exhibit 4.

---

[1] "D.C. Plan Asset Allocation Profiles," *IOMA Report on Defined Contribution Investing* (January 28, 1997): 28.

Exhibit 4: Synthetic GIC Issuers and Wrapped Assets Outstanding as of December 31, 1995

Insurance Companies	$
Providian	12,122,000,000
AIG Financial	2,500,000,000
Transamerica	620,000,000
Security Life of Denver	614,143,652
Prudential	222,600,000
Allmerica	96,000,000
Jackson National	94,000,000
Other	902,000,000
Subtotal	**$17,170,743,652**
Banks	$
Bankers Trust	14,000,000,000
JP Morgan	5,500,000,000
Union Bank Switzerland	4,000,000,000
National Westminster	2,700,000,000
CDC Investment	2,520,000,000
Deutsche Bank	2,150,000,000
Rabobank	1,600,000,000
State Street	1,558,000,000
Chase Manhattan	1,300,000,000
Westdeutsche Landesbank	500,000,000
Barclays Bank	340,000,000
Subtotal	**$36,168,000,000**
Total	**$53,338,743,652**

Source: Galliard Capital Management

STABLE-VALUE PORTFOLIO MANAGEMENT

Stable-value portfolio management has changed dramatically in recent years as the combination of innovative products and new providers has virtually redefined how portfolios are structured and managed. The increased use of GIC alternatives such as synthetics has advanced portfolio management to the point where most traditional bond management strategies can be emulated within stable-value portfolios, while maintaining the low return volatility characteristics of stable value through book-value wrappers. In fact, major bond market participants such as multinational banks, securities dealers, and fixed-income managers have been at the forefront of product development and industry change as they have sought ways to apply their expertise to a market which, until recently, had been dominated by insurance companies.

This section highlights some general considerations in managing the traditional stable-value portfolio, with an emphasis on the use of synthetics. It also discusses some of the relevant contract terms and considerations impacting the portfolio structuring process.

Stable-Value Portfolio Objectives

Consistent with the role of stable value as the safe option in most defined contribution plans today, the overriding objective in managing these portfolios is preservation of principal. Liquidity to meet participant withdrawals is an additional factor, as is earning a fairly stable return which exceeds that of shorter-maturity alternatives. Portfolio management strategies should address these objectives and should guide the selection of individual issues.

Credit Quality

All holdings in a stable-value portfolio — whether traditional GICs/BICs, wrap contracts, or assets underlying wrap contracts — must be high-quality instruments. A stringent credit review process is used initially to review issuers and to monitor them on an ongoing basis. Most managers establish minimum credit quality rating standards of single-A or double-A and require that the overall quality rating of the portfolio exceed Aa3 as measured by Moody's Investors Service or AA– by Standard & Poor's. Synthetic GICs can improve portfolio credit quality, since their underlying securities are often obligations of the U.S. government or its agencies, well structured mortgage/asset-backed securities, or highly rated corporate bonds. Investors must look deeper than the financial statements and the opinions of the rating agencies, however. Factors including the issuer's mix of business, amount of leverage, investment portfolio structure and liquidity, and the breadth and depth of management must also be explored.

Diversification

Diversification is a critical element in any portfolio management process and was a particularly thorny issue in stable-value portfolios prior to the advent of synthetics. Fiduciaries of employee benefit plans are charged with adequately diversifying portfolios under ERISA to minimize the risk of large losses. It could be argued that many stable-value portfolios historically did not fulfill this obligation because they were exposed almost entirely to financial services companies, often with large exposures to single issuers. As discussed earlier, defaults in the early 1990s drew attention to the diversification issue, however, and led to the propagation of synthetics.

Prudent diversification standards limit portfolio assets invested in a single issuer to no more than 10%. Most fixed-income practitioners limit holdings of non-U.S. government issues to no more than 5% and broadly diversify among different fixed-income sectors, industries, and security types. A similar result can be achieved in stable-value portfolios by looking through to the securities underlying synthetics. Traditional GICs/BICs should be viewed as an important sector of the portfolio, but limited by industry diversification guidelines similar to other holdings.

Diversification constraints should be measured according to the net exposure to an individual issuer or sector. For contract issuers, full principal exposure of traditional issues and the difference between the market and book values of their synthetic contracts should be totaled. Likewise, credit exposure is measured for all underlying holdings. A well-diversified stable-value portfolio is portrayed in exhibits 5 and 6. As shown, diversification is properly measured at both the aggregate portfolio and underlying security levels.

Maturity Structure

The maturity structure of stable-value portfolios must ensure that liquidity is adequate for meeting participant withdrawals. Generally, a buffer of available cash equal to at least 5% of the portfolio is invested in a stable-value collective fund, a money market fund, or other liquid, short-term instruments. Individual portfolio holdings are then structured with longer maturities to provide funds at regular intervals. Laddering the portfolio in this fashion assures that funds are available to accommodate liquidity needs and reinvest at current market rates. Portfolio maturity structures are typically short, averaging two to three years, with the longest holdings rarely exceeding five to seven years.

Synthetic contracts, however, have greatly improved the flexibility in portfolio maturity structuring, since the underlying securities are highly marketable. Liquidity may be constrained if the underlying securities' market value is significantly below their book value. When market value is near book value or higher, however, the portfolio manager is more able to meet unusual withdrawal requirements or shift the composition of the portfolio.

When structuring maturities, actively managed synthetics with constant durations must be factored into the equation. The average maturity of each active portfolio may be used as a proxy for the contract's maturity. However, managed contracts neither mature nor provide cash-flow contributions within the broader portfolio structure.

Exhibit 5: Hypothetical Stable-Value Portfolio

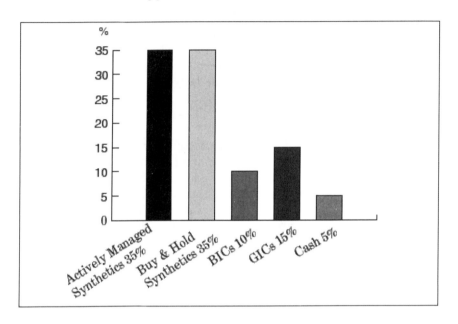

Exhibit 6: Hypothetical Stable-Value Portfolio

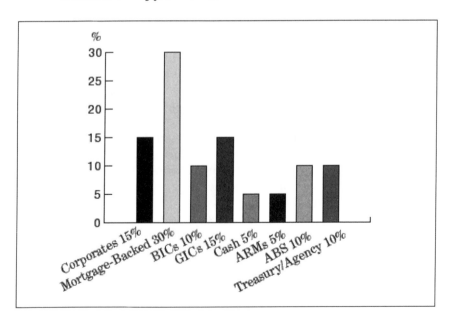

Duration and Convexity

Previously, the exclusive use of traditional GICs precluded the need to understand duration or convexity. However, the use of synthetics requires portfolio managers to track the duration characteristics of the securities underlying synthetics within a stable-value fund. Sophisticated analytical systems are required for this effort. Again, given the principal protection objective of stable-value funds, the volatility of underlying securities should be consistent with a two- to three-year average maturity. Volatility measurement is especially important when securities that possess various cash-flow characteristics, such as mortgage passthrough or mortgage/asset-backed securities are used. Guidelines must be established for active managers to assure that the use of higher-risk mortgage securities is limited. The negative convexity in these instruments can dramatically affect cash flows, which impacts the market value of the underlying portfolio and, thus, the crediting rate of the contract.

Asset Allocation Among Synthetic Structures

Portfolio strategies devised at the aggregate portfolio level must specify the allocation levels for different types of synthetic contracts as well as different issuers. No specific formula for allocation exists, for it depends upon the manager's level of comfort with synthetics, as well as his or her expertise. One approach is, first, to determine allocations to cash and traditional contracts, then allocate remaining assets to synthetic structures with a balance between buy-and-hold and actively managed contracts. The buy-and-hold structures provide cash flow to the broader portfolio and should be structured with portfolio guidelines for credit quality, diversification, and maturity in mind.

Actively managed synthetics are structured to achieve certain return objectives, but must also comply with the aggregate portfolio guidelines. A benchmark is commonly selected and management guidelines are established relative to this bogey. The amount of latitude given to investment managers should be carefully considered. Wrap providers that are liable for the shortfalls incurred when a portfolio's market value drops below book value will typically limit the investment manager's ability to move the portfolio's duration away from its benchmark. Wrap providers also limit, if not ban completely, the use of higher-risk securities, which allows them to quantify potential liabilities and contain risk.

Portfolio Management — Another View

More recently, larger plan sponsors have taken a less traditional approach in managing their stable-value portfolios, choosing to view them in a way that is more similar to their other fixed-income options, only with a book-value wrapper. This allocation strategy involves hiring one or more active fixed-income managers for the fund, each with a particular area of expertise or style, to manage actively all of the assets in the plan option — similar to the way they would structure their marketable bond fund or their defined-benefit plan fixed-income portfolio. The plan sponsor then secures one or more book-value wrapper agreements to provide for portfolio valuations at book.

Each manager must adhere to a set of investment guidelines agreed upon with the plan sponsor and wrap provider. The sponsor may maintain a liquidity reserve for payment of normal plan benefit payments to reduce the likelihood of book-value payments from the active synthetic contracts.

If the plan's cash flow history has consistently been positive, the plan sponsor may retain little or no reserve. But the sponsor will be required by the wrap provider to purchase only experience-rated (participating) contracts, so that any shortfall between the market value of the portfolio and book value in the event of a payout will be recovered from the plan rather than absorbed by the wrap provider.

Contract Considerations

Given that there are no industry standards governing the various types of stable-value contracts, they may vary materially from one issuer to another. As such, a thorough contract review is imperative and should be completed prior to the contract's final execution. All contracts will have terms dealing with the legal representations and warranties of the parties as well as provisions relating to the calculation of the credited rate of interest; contract withdrawals; terminations, including formulae for market-value adjustment; and the hierarchy for withdrawals within the total plan (that is, pro rata or LIFO).

Synthetic contracts are more complex, requiring additional provisions relating to the treatment of any losses realized from the liquidation of the underlying securities in the event of a withdrawal or termination. Synthetic contracts may be experience rated or non-experience rated (also called participating or nonparticpating). If experience rated, any losses realized from security sales to fund a withdrawal would be borne by the plan and recovered through a lower crediting rate of interest to participants. For non-experience-rated contracts, the risk of loss is borne by the issuer. As might be expected, non-experience-rated contracts have a somewhat higher fee than experience-rated contracts to compensate the issuer for the additional risk.

THE FUTURE OF STABLE VALUE

The tremendous change occurring recently in stable-value products, providers, and strategies will continue to reshape the market in coming years. While aggregate industry assets will more than likely experience only modest growth until the long-awaited retirement of baby boomers begins sometime around the year 2007, significant shifts will continue within the market in terms of product use and development, portfolio management strategies, and the players themselves. This section briefly highlights some of the market's major trends and provides some thoughts about the future.

From a product standpoint, pooled funds and actively managed synthetics are likely to continue to experience solid growth at the expense of traditional GICs, the use of which is expected to decline further. Separate account GICs will be utilized, but to a lesser extent than synthetics. Fixed-income managers are the clear beneficiary of the movement to managed synthetics and they will continue to play a bigger and bigger role in the marketplace. Indeed, one of the more interesting developments to watch will be the vanishing distinction between fixed-income managers and stable-value managers.

For the stable-value asset manager, market growth in the immediate future will largely be attained by successfully capturing other segments of the defined-contribution market, such as public deferred compensation plans (457) and retirement plans for tax-exempt organizations (403[b]). These sectors are just beginning to follow the corporate market in offering more diversified stable-value options including synthetic GICs and pooled funds at the expense of bank savings vehicles and fixed annuities.

Product innovations are continuing, as well. The SEC recently registered a stable-value fund for the first time. The mutual fund provides a professionally managed, well diversified fund in a format that is popular with participants, providing them with the ability to track their investments daily in the newspapers together with "portability" at retirement. Innovations continue as well within synthetic structures, including wrapping of specialized fixed-income styles and other asset classes such as high-yield, international bonds, and even equities.

While these newer structures are still a comparatively small part of the market, the quest for higher yields is beginning to manifest itself in riskier strategies. Plan sponsors must take care to understand all of the strategies that are utilized in their stable-value option and make sure they are comfortable that appropriate risk levels are maintained given the objective of principal preservation stated for this investment option.

On the issuer side, wrap fees have continued to plummet as these contracts have virtually become commoditized. Fees for wrapper agreements are averaging 12 to 15 basis points, and many deals have been struck at lower levels. It is likely that continued declines in wrap fees will cause consolidation on the issuer side of the industry, with the emergence of a few very large players.

A final trend that is being promoted within the industry relates to stable value as a distinct asset class, highly efficient in terms of risk and return. With attractive yields and low volatility of returns, many in the industry are beginning to recommend stable value as a substitute in balanced funds for traditional bond portfolios. Given the higher risk-adjusted returns, investors could reduce risk (volatility) in their portfolios by utilizing stable value in place of marketable bonds. Likewise, investors could increase their exposure to equities and improve expected returns while maintaining the same level of return volatility by utilizing stable value in balanced account options.

Whether stable value becomes a staple in balanced account strategies remains to be seen. What is clear is that participants applaud the high-return/low-volatility nature of stable-value investments and will likely continue to allocate a large portion of their fixed-income investments to this asset class in the future.

InformationManagementNetwork

Frank J. Frank J. Fabozzi/Information Management Network provides quality educational programs for the global investment community. IMN's annual schedule includes domestic and international investment management events in Asia, the Caribbean, Europe, North America, and South America. In its fifth year of operations, Frank J. Fabozzi/IMN has taken the leadership position with conferences attracting over 7,500 senior executives.

Calendar of Events for 1999

January	Asset Allocation	Palm Springs, CA
	Stable-Value Symposium	New York, NY
	Fixed-Income Summit	New York, NY
	Hedge Fund Investors' Summit	Phoenix, AZ
February	Securities Lending	Phoenix, AZ
	Leveraged Loans & High-Yield Debt	New York, NY
	World Cup of Indexing™	Zurich, Switzerland
March	Public Fund Boards Summit	Phoenix, AZ
April	Risk Management	To Be Announced
	Corporate Pension Funds	TBA, Florida
May	Cash Management	TBA
June	Private Equity	New York, NY
	Fire & Police Pension Plans	Lake Tahoe, NV
	West Coast Endowments & Foundations	San Francisco, CA
September	Institutional Investment Management Summit	TBA
	Finance & Investment for Hospitals & Healthcare Systems	New York, NY
November	Private Placements	New York, NY

For more information or to request brochures, please call **Information Management Network** at (212) 768-2800 ext. 1

AW
1:10 → 2:43

SLC → BOS → AMS
1970

10AM – 4:34 · 1728.50

S	M	T	W	Th	Fr	Sc
14	15	16	17	18	19	20
X	X	PHO	SLC	SLC	SLC	SLC
21	22	23	24	25	26	27
BOS	BOS	AMS	AMS	AMS	AMS	TXRCRS
28	29	30	31	1	2	3
TXRSd	DEP	DEP	DEP			

B. Borden
P. Gerlings
NIC.

26 - Dinner
LASSRS
NO FIRE
D.R
Peter
Nicole